AF572012

FROM THE LIBRARY OF
ALAN JAMES ROBINSON

The Changing World of Birds

a changing world book

Illustrated with photographs

Holt, Rinehart and Winston, Inc.
New York Chicago San Francisco

The Changing World of Birds

By John M. Anderson

To my wife, Nancy Jane, for many contributions.

Acknowledgments

All the pictures in this book are from the National Audubon Society. The following people took the photographs: G. Ronald Austing, pages 24, 34; Mark Boulton, pages *iii*, 30, 69; Allan D. Cruickshank, pages 5, 19, 29, 48, 99; Ron Curbow, page 73; Thase Daniel, page 87; Jack Dermid, page 58; Grant Haist, page *vi*; Haverschmidt, page 63; Eric Hosking, page 67; Ray Hunold, page 101; William J. Jahoda, page 35; George Komorowski, page 32, Karl H. Maslowski, pages 6, 17; D. Muir, page 44; Mrs. Wm. H. Phelps, Jr., page 15; Leonard Lee Rue III, pages 12, 38; Hugo Schroder, page 60; Alvin E. Staffan, page 46; M. F. Soper, page 27; John K. Terres, page 83; Jack White, page 3; Robert H. Wright, page 76.

 Published simultaneously in Canada by Holt, Rinehart and Winston of Canada, Limited. ISBN: 0-03-091301-2 (Trade) • ISBN: 0-03-091302-0 (HLE) • Library of Congress Catalog Card Number: 75-182780 • Printed in the United States of America • First Edition
Designed by Aileen Friedman

contents

These seagulls have made Mohawk Island in Lake Erie their habitat.

Habitat

chapter one

When you wake up in the morning, smell breakfast, and hear other members of your family, you are at home. At home, you feel safe. But, if you had to go to the opposite side of town to eat, through neighborhoods full of unfriendly strangers, you would not like that situation.

A bird that wakens at dawn may not find breakfast next to the roosting site where it spent the night. If so, it has to go and search for food. If it is a bobwhite quail, a pheasant, or a song sparrow, the bird searches the ground for weed seeds such as ragweed or foxtail grass seeds. If a hungry hawk is perched in a tree nearby, the bobwhite does not dare walk across open ground to get to its food. The bobwhite looks for a brushy fence row, or a stretch of wetland in which grass and cattails grow. Then it walks beneath the branches and tall grass, hidden from its sharp-eyed enemy, the hawk.

The hawk in this case is a predator, seeking to kill and to eat its prey, the bobwhite. While eating or searching for food, the quail cannot afford to be exposed to hawks or other predators such as foxes, owls, or cats for very long.

It is obvious that the habitat, or land on which the bird lives, must provide the bird with a safe place to eat, a supply of food, a safe place to sleep, and safe travel lanes in which to move about. These and many other features must be available every day of the year. If the bird does not migrate from one region to another, the area where it lives must provide its every need the year around.

In contrast to birds that remain in one place throughout the four seasons, some species spend the summer in far northern climes such as Alaska or Greenland and spend the winter near the equator. But the need for food and for shelter from enemies and the elements is ever-present, whether the bird is migrating, wintering, nesting, or rearing young.

The changes people make around the world affect the land's ability to meet the needs of birds in many ways. A little more than one hundred years ago, for example, Americans must have felt that there was plenty of land for everybody. In New England fences were usually made of stones piled in a row, and in the Midwest, wooden rails were laid in a zig-zag fence line. When the farmers plowed, they left several feet on either side of the fences where brush and grasses grew. Crevices between the stones provided homes for wrens; holes in the wooden posts and rails were occupied by bluebirds; shrubs, weeds, and grass along both sides afforded food, shelter, and safe passage for many kinds of wildlife.

Along ditches and small streams the farmer also allowed natural vegetation to grow because he knew heavy rains would cause the streams to rise and flood these strips of land. It was useless, in fact, impossible, to plant corn on land that would be under water for two weeks or more in the springtime. Although the farmer did not plow his fence rows or his wetlands in bygone days, he did not worry about the unused space because there was more land than he or his neighbors could use. Whether he meant to do so or not, the farmer provided excellent food and shelter for birds.

Today, farmers have ditches to drain the water from small ponds and marshes in most of the United States. They have replaced the rail fences with one single strand of electric wire. When a cow or a deer touches this wire, it gets an electric shock. This frightens the animal away; so a fence of stones or rails is not necessary to keep it out of the fields. Because the farmer does not need to leave a wide lane for a fence, and now wants to use every acre of ground, he plows right up to the electric wire. This leaves no brush or weeds for birds to live in. Over

Bare ground offers no food or shelter for birds.

much of their range, the ground-dwelling birds have had the lanes blocked between their sleeping, resting, and feeding places. They can no longer live where this has happened.

Some long-distance fliers such as blue herons, who are fish eaters, may roost in the tops of tall trees and then fly a mile or more to feeding grounds. Wild ducks and geese usually feed on plants that grow in water or in nearby grain fields. They are seldom very far from water when sleeping or eating. When people drain or poison marshes, lakes, and rivers, it means the end of fish-eating or aquatic plant-eating birds.

Still other birds such as purple martins, swallows, chimney swifts, and whippoorwills feed by catching insects in midair. Clean air and flying insects which are not carrying poisonous pesticides are necessary in any area where these birds live.

At nesting time, the different kinds of birds seek specific kinds of habitat in which to make nests and lay eggs. If suitable conditions cannot be found, the birds may not try to reproduce. Sometimes acceptable nesting conditions may encourage the parents to nest, but the environment may be changed so drastically, either before or after hatching, that the eggs or young are destroyed. A mallard on the northern prairies, for example, may lay its eggs in wheat stubble which is plowed up before hatching, or in a marsh, which is then drained. If such events occur too often, the species declines in numbers or may even become extinct.

Another case in point is the wood stork, or wood ibis

as they are sometimes called. These big wading birds nest in great colonies in swamps in the southeastern United States and eastern Mexico. Swamps have a mixture of trees or shrubs growing in water. The Corkscrew Swamp in Florida is the largest virgin cypress swamp left in America. It is occupied by 3000 to 6000 pairs of wood storks. During a drought, the swamp and surrounding areas may dry up. Although wood storks nest in the swamp, they feed the young on fish which the adult birds catch in nearby marshes and ponds. Food is usually plentiful in marshy areas where cattails, bulrushes, and other plants without woody stems grow.

In nesting season the wood stork needs concentrated, abundant supplies of fish.

When the marshes go dry, there is no food for nestling storks. The adult birds could fly to far-off marshes in search of food, but would be unable to carry a mouthful of fish all the way back to the cypress swamp to feed the nestlings. Instead, when there is a drought, the wood storks simply refuse to make nests and to lay eggs that year.

At the other extreme, an unusual amount of rainfall may inundate a swamp area and most of the surrounding countryside. Fish then leave the confines of the pond and spread throughout the wetlands. If this happens during the nesting season, as it did in Florida in 1970, young storks perish because fish are not concentrated in ponds and the adult storks cannot catch large quantities with a single dip of their huge beaks.

Trees, water, and fish, free from pesticides, are essential if the bald eagle is to survive.

Unlike the stork, an eagle returns every year to the same nest, usually in the top of a tall tree, and adds more sticks to it. The nests become so large that they can be seen for miles and may weigh more than a ton. Except for men who may cut down the tree or shoot the parent birds, the eagles have few natural enemies and little to fear from periods of dry or rainy weather. Therefore, as long as there are enough big trees near water and fish that are not contaminated, America's national emblem, the bald eagle, should survive.

The pheasant, on the other hand, must hide its nest from crows, skunks, foxes, raccoons, and great horned owls. It makes its nest on the ground, hidden in tall grass. When there were rail fences, the pheasant often nested in the grass and briars along the fence. Today, it often resorts to hayfields where the bird and its nest are in danger of being cut to pieces by the farmer's mowing machine.

Changes in the environment of various birds force them either to move to other areas in search of suitable living conditions or to die. Upon moving to a new area, the bird usually finds all the suitable nesting habitat already occupied by others of the same species. This makes adjustment more difficult.

Environments of all creatures all over the world have been gradually changing since the earth began. Some creatures could neither adjust nor migrate, and the only proof of their former existence lies in their fossil remains, found in rocks.

For example, half a billion years ago, in what geologists call the Cambrian Period, there were no birds. Warm shallow seas covered the central part of what is now North America. As the continent gradually rose or sank, the seas retreated or advanced. As they did so, sediments were deposited on the sea floor, and these later solidified into rock.

Radioactive materials found in rock break down into lighter elements at a constant rate, like a clock's ticking. Geologists can measure how much of the lighter elements are present in a rock and determine from that how long the breaking-down process has been going on. In this way, they can tell accurately the age of rocks in which fossil remains of birds are found.

Near the end of the Pennsylvanian Period, about 225 million years ago, rocks were formed which contain skeletons of giant reptiles. Unlike any animals before them, some of these reptiles were able to live entirely on land. Some reptiles possessed featherlike membranes which enabled them to glide through the air for short distances. These reptiles were probably the ancestors of modern birds.

About two million years ago, temperatures dropped around the world. Great ice caps formed in the northern regions, spread southward, and then melted back northward at least four different times. The period in which these great ice sheets, or glaciers, advanced and retreated is called the Pleistocene epoch. It lasted until about 10,000 years ago, by which time most modern bird forms had evolved. In other words, when the last glacier melted, there were about the same number of kinds of birds as there are today.

Some bird species apparently preferred the cold climate and probably followed the glacier as it retreated northward. To this day, these birds live in the land of the midnight sun known as the Arctic. Other bird species apparently settled in tropical climes where the temperature never drops below the comfort zone. Still others migrate with the changing seasons—going north in spring, south in autumn.

Each species, however, must find its own special living requirements every day of the year. It is adapted to these special conditions and cannot survive unless it finds them. Although enormous changes have taken place in the geologic past, men now make more environmental changes in a decade than formerly happened in millions of years. People drain marshes, flood valleys, cut forests, plow the prairie, and kill plants, birds, mammals, and insects in a variety of ways. Can birds adjust to these changes?

Because birds provide much of the food people eat, protect plants from insects, and enrich human life in many ways, people depend on them.

Just as a thermometer shows when the temperature is comfortable, healthy birdlife shows when the environment is healthy, both for birds and for people. A sudden decline in any bird population is a strong indicator that that environment is changing in a way that may be harmful to people, too.

For this reason, men try to provide suitable habitat for birds. Much is known about what birds need for survival, but if men are to survive, they must keep a watchful eye on the changing environment of birds.

Nesting and Rearing Young

chapter two

A mammal, such as a muskrat or a human being, develops from an egg that is fertilized within the body of the mother. The fertilized egg, or embryo, grows within the mother's body until the baby mammal is ready to be born.

Not so with birds. The egg is fertilized within the female, just as in mammals, but the embryo is then enclosed in a hard shell and passes out of the body through a tube called the oviduct. A chicken's egg "laid" in this manner may be taken to the grocery store and then to a person's breakfast table. Inside the shell is the yellow yolk and a white fluid called albumen. These nutritious elements make up an important part of the diet for many egg eaters other than people.

If an egg is fertilized by a sperm and is not eaten by other animals, the yolk and albumen become food for the bird embryo, which grows inside the shell until it is ready to hatch. There is a tiny tooth on top of a bird's bill, which an infant bird uses to saw its way out of its egg and into a totally new environment.

From the time of hatching, a bird must find or be supplied with its food. Its parents or its own feathers must keep the bird warm. It must be protected from enemies and, eventually, it must produce more of its kind.

At any time or place, a bird's environment consists of a combination of temperature, moisture, soil, plants, and other animals. That combination of environmental factors must be just right, or the bird will not survive in that place.

While an embryo is developing, the egg must be kept warm and moist. It must also be turned over about once a day. These incubation chores are sometimes shared by both parent birds, as in the case of bald eagles, which take turns sitting on the eggs. In other cases, one parent assumes all care of the eggs. This is true of many kinds of ducks—the drake abandons its mate long before the eggs hatch and does not return.

The phalarope, a bird that inhabits shorelines, has a different life style. The female phalarope lays her eggs and leaves the male to incubate them until they hatch. The male then has to raise the brood of young phalaropes by himself. Other species, such as wild geese, may share the responsibility for raising the young, but the goose does all the incubating while the gander stands guard nearby.

The environment in which a bird builds its nest must provide material for nest building, food, and shelter for both parent birds and young, and protection from egg eaters. Some species build very elaborate nests, while others, such as terns and penguins, may settle for a bare spot in the sand. In either case, the environment must provide the materials for the kind of habitat that a particular species requires.

Several kinds of ducks, such as the common goldeneye, nest in holes in trees. Unlike woodpeckers, ducks are not equipped with chisel beaks and cannot peck holes in trees. Therefore, they must either find trees with suitable holes or boxes which people erect for them to use. These ducks do not carry sticks or grass for nesting material but will use wood chips or sawdust in a hollow tree or box. When the female duck is off her nest, the eggs are kept warm by a layer of fluffy down feathers pulled from her breast.

In contrast to those hole nesters, which carry no materials and build no nest, many species do both. A Baltimore oriole, for example, fastens its nest to the tips of

The Baltimore oriole weaves an elaborate nest on the tips of tree branches.

branches and weaves an elaborate hanging cradle that sways in the breeze. Each thread of hair and leaf of grass the bird uses, it finds nearby and carries to the nest. A favorite tree for oriole nesting is the American elm, which is being wiped out over most of its range by Dutch elm disease. It is hoped that the oriole can nest in maples, willows, and other trees just as well. Where trees of all kinds are replaced by houses, factories, airports, and roads, the tree-nesting Baltimore oriole must disappear.

An oriolelike bird in the tropics, the oropendola, is a champion among nest builders. It weaves a marvelous grass stocking from 3 to 6 feet long, with an entrance at the top and a cradle at the bottom. Each pair of oropendolas makes a separate nest, but many pairs occupy the same tree, forming a colony.

The social weaverbird of South Africa, another colonial nester, builds an apartment house with over 100 chambers. The entire structure, made of straws and grass, hangs high in the branches of a sturdy tree and may be 10 feet high and 15 feet in diameter, larger than the houses of nearby human residents. This massive dwelling, which, unlike oriole nests, is occupied throughout the year, is built by birds no bigger than the common house sparrow. Social weavers and house sparrows are both members of a large family of birds known as weaver finches.

America's house sparrow is often called the English sparrow because the first few pairs were brought over from England and released in a cemetery in Brooklyn, New York, in 1852. Starting with these few, the species has since spread across the entire continent. The house sparrow has followed European civilization all over the world. It is the most successful city and town dweller of all birds. Its nest is an untidy bulk of straw, twigs, feathers, and trash—always domed, with a side entrance when out in the open. A hole in a building, a ledge under the eaves, or a crevice among rocks serves the house sparrow equally well as a nest shelter. Thus, when people cut forests to erect buildings, it is at the expense of the Baltimore oriole but to the advantage of the house sparrow—a change most bird lovers would rather not see take place because house sparrows compete with other more desirable species. Man makes an environmental change by replacing forest with buildings; this brings about an increase in house sparrows. The sparrows themselves then become an environmental factor limiting the numbers of bluebirds. This shows how a change in one environmental factor starts a chain reaction, causing other changes.

Nesting in great colonies is a trait common to a wide variety of birds from swallows to flamingos.

Flamingos build mounds, usually between 6 and 18 inches high and one foot in diameter, with a basin-shaped nest on top. The nests are usually built in salty or alkaline shallow lakes. Flamingos are long-legged, long-necked, wading birds with peculiar beaks shaped like small scoop shovels turned upside down. Thus equipped, flamingos scoop up nesting material consisting of soft mud which soon hardens into a nest mound. There the female flamingo lays a single egg.

Nesting and Rearing Young

As soon as the downy feathers on newly hatched flamingos dry, they are able to swim. As a rule, however, the birds stay in the nest for three or four days. During this period, the young are fed a pabulumlike mixture from the beaks of their parents. As yet, no one knows exactly what this baby food is or how the parent birds make it.

After leaving the nest, young flamingos swim and wade about the shallow lakes in large flocks. A few adult birds may accompany and feed the flock (sometimes called a *crèche*) for a few weeks until the young can forage on their own.

Flamingos build mounds of mud with a basin-shaped nest on top.

Slits on the flamingo's upper bill and a comblike structure on the big tongue function as a pump and sieve through which food particles are screened out of the muddy water. With this peculiar beak, the flamingo has a special tool for eating and nest-building. At the same time, this equipment means that the flamingo can only live where it finds a particular combination of water, chemicals such as salt or soda, and the plants and few other animals that can live in that harsh environment.

Actually there is no scientific evidence that flamingos *need* salt and/or soda in order to survive. But these birds have been able to adapt to the harsh environments where these chemicals exist and have lived in such places for centuries. Because few other organisms can tolerate such chemicals, the flamingos have relatively little competition for the available food supply and the land and water areas.

The Morton Salt Company, on the island of Inagua in the Bahamas, is well aware that the big, pink birds are inseparable from salt flats. On this tropical isle, where salt is produced by evaporating sea water, flamingos are carefully protected from hunters by Great Britain through the Bahamas National Trust, by the United States through the Audubon Society, and by the Morton Salt Company. These agencies are also studying the flamingo in order to avoid changing the environment in any way that would be to the flamingos' disadvantage.

What a contrast between a young flamingo, that shifts for itself soon after it is born, and a young bald eagle that stays in its nest, eating fish, birds, and small mammals brought by its parents. Young eagles are fed in this manner until they grow as large, or larger, than their parents, which takes about four months.

Equipped with sharp, powerful talons and hooked beaks, adult eagles cut and tear the flesh of their prey into pieces small enough for their young to swallow. Bald eagles are about a month old before they are strong enough to feed themselves in the nest.

Once the young eagle leaves the nest and becomes a fledgling, it has few enemies except man. Many eagles are shot by hunters and sheepherders who claim eagles devour their lambs. But an even greater threat lies in fish which have eaten insects carrying poison and, in turn, poison the eagles that eat them.

Young bald eagles are fed in the nest until they are as large as their parents.

The life of a young partridge is different. It leaves the nest with the rest of the brood as soon as its downy feathers are dry. It follows its mother about the landscape, learning to catch insects, to find weed seeds, and to seek shelter from predators. Its predators consist of hawks, owls, wildcats, foxes, minks, and weasels. In fact, the life of a young partridge is so hazardous that less than half of each partidge brood survives.

Most songbirds such as thrushes, finches, and warblers are altricial like the eagle. This means that they are born helpless, blind, almost naked, and that they stay in the nest until they are big enough to fly. Unlike eagles, however, young songbirds face many enemies. Only a few of them escape the predators, automobiles, violent winds, rain, and hail that confront them.

In considering the many different families of birds with their different environmental needs, it should be kept in mind that birds were well adjusted to life on various continents long before men came on the scene. As men gradually occupied one region after another, they made changes which wiped out some birds but benefited others.

In North America, tremendous flocks of passenger pigeons once nested over many square miles of hardwood forests. As these forests gave way to agriculture, the pigeons lost their ancestral nesting ground and became extinct in 1914. The hunter's gun may have hastened the process, but passenger pigeons would undoubtedly still be part of the American landscape if their nesting environment had not been so drastically changed.

The wild chicken of the Atlantic states, called the heath hen, once occupied sandy ridges and extensive, uncultivated lands covered with low-growing scrub oak, pines, and shrubs. Cultivation and human habitation of these areas brought the demise of the heath hen. The last known specimen disppeared from Martha's Vineyard, an island off Massachusetts, in 1932.

In Germany and Poland, on the other hand, the white stork, which formerly nested in rocky cliffs and trees, adjusted to nesting on housetops in rural villages. Barn swallows, American robins, and Chinese pheasants are some other examples of birds that are probably more numerous in America today than before the advent of European settlers. In contrast, today only a remnant flock of whooping cranes and prairie grouse are struggling to survive in a changing world, as the marshlands and prairies give way to agriculture.

A whooping crane. Only about sixty of these birds have survived the changes in their environment.

As Dr. Roger Tory Peterson, world-famous ornithologist and artist, pointed out, birds could do very well without people. But, without birds, life for most people would be intolerable.

Mosquitoes, for example, in many places have become immune to all known chemical pesticides, but they are not immune to the army of birds that feeds on insects. In addition, a recent survey shows some 10 million people in the United States alone who list bird-watching as their favorite hobby.

People must remember that marsh birds cannot survive without marshes; sea birds cannot feed their young in oily waters; forest birds cannot live in a land of cities and farms. Man can live in marshes, prairies, oceans, deserts, and man can live in cities and on farms. But these areas must be maintained in such a way that birds, as well as other wild creatures, can live there, too. The disappearance of birds from any environment is a warning signal to man.

Adaptations of Birds

chapter three

If one finds a nest of eggs, the egg layer very likely was a bird. But if one took the eggs to a biologist, claiming they *prove* there are birds nearby, the scientist might well ask, "Why couldn't this be the work of a turtle or an alligator, since many reptiles lay eggs?" Even the duck-billed platypus, a kind of rare mammal found in Australia, lays eggs.

If one added that there was something flying near the nest, he might point out that it could have been a bat or a large flying insect. Birds are the best but by no means the world's *only* fliers. But if one could produce a feather as evidence, then no one could deny that it could have come only from a bird.

Smooth scales on birds' feet and legs are a clue that they evolved from reptiles. One might even argue that the rest of the bird's body is covered with scales because feathers evolved from them, too. A feather is, therefore, a very elaborate scale.

The different kinds of feathers serve birds and people in various ways. In the days of King George III and Benjamin Franklin, people used *contour* feathers when writing. The hollow central shaft with the round, bare quill at the lower end made a fairly good writing instrument when dipped in ink. American Indians used contour feathers, usually from the bald eagle's white tail, to make war bonnets. On a bird, contour feathers are the ones that cover the back and sides of the body and most of the wings.

On either side of the shaft of a contour feather is the vane, which is composed of hundreds of tiny, parallel threads called *barbs*. Barbs are hooked to each other by thousands of tiny barbules equipped with microscopic hooks. If the barbs split apart, the bird can hook them back together by drawing that feather through its bill, an action quite like that of a zipper.

Down feathers are bits of fluff usually hidden beneath the contour feathers. Most down feathers lack a stiff central shaft, and the barbules lack hooks so the stiff vane of a contour feather is missing from them.

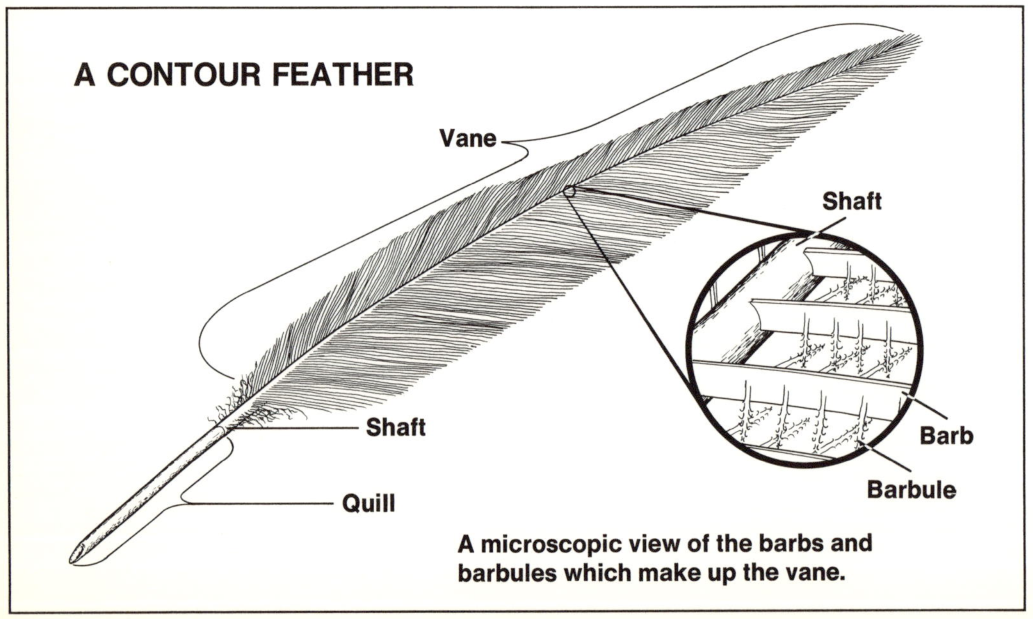

A microscopic view of the barbs and barbules which make up the vane.

This fluffy, insulated layer of down, covered by airtight, waterproof contour feathers, keeps birds warm. It kept them warm during the glacial periods thousands of years before man learned to use the same materials for the same purpose.

The eider duck of Iceland, like most of its relatives, lines its nest with down pulled from the female's breast. Eider down is famous around the world as a stuffing for pillows, sleeping bags, and clothing. In Iceland, where eider ducks are strictly protected, some people work as "down farmers." These farmers have learned that a female eider duck can produce enough down for about one and a half nests. Each year, when the duck starts to nest, the farmers take part of the down which the duck replaces. After the ducklings are hatched and gone, the down collector returns and gathers the rest of the down.

Owls have down feathers covering the contour feathers on the top of their wings. This enables them to fly silently through the night and to swoop down upon an unsuspecting rabbit or mouse. In contrast, the bare contour feathers on the wings of the common goldeneye duck make such a noise when these birds fly that they are often called "whistlers."

The tiny "hairs" called *filoplumes,* left on the body of a plucked chicken or turkey, represent another kind of feather. These occur in circles around the base of contour feathers. Their function is unknown.

Most feathers are shed or *molted* and replaced by new ones at least once or twice each year. Molting is usually gradual, so there are enough feathers on the wings to permit flight. The ducks and geese, however, shed the contour feathers on the wings, known as *primaries,* all at one time. Thus, they are temporarily flightless every summer.

Another type of feather found on the bellies of herons, bitterns, parrots, and hawks is not molted but grows continuously at the base. At the outer end, they continuously disintegrate, forming a fine talcumlike powder which waterproofs the other feathers,

Most birds waterproof their feathers by rubbing their beaks across an oil gland near the tail and wiping the oil on their feathers. This action is called *preening.*

Creatures that fly as fast or as far as birds must have the most efficient and most lightweight covering and skeleton. Feathers as a cover make for lightness, while being the strongest materials for their size and weight known. The bird skeleton has fewer bones than the hu-

The primary feathers in a bobwhite's wings bend upward as the bird rises from the ground like a rocket.

man skeleton, and these bones are hollow, thin, and flat. Birds are also light because air spaces occur in their lungs and body cavities. No heavy jaws of teeth weigh down a flying bird. Instead of teeth, birds have a grinding organ called the *gizzard* near the center of their body where it does not upset the flier's balance. Feathers also streamline the body, smoothing over the angles, even providing a pocket for the feet, or landing gear, in most birds.

While feathers bear no resemblance to reptilian scales, the feet and legs of birds are covered with scales quite similar to those on a snake.

Human toenails may not seem very useful. In some birds, however, the tendons in their feet automatically lock their toes around branches whenever they go to sleep. Sharp toenails or claws enable some species to climb trees or cling to the underside of horizontal branches. The claws or talons of eagles, hawks, and owls are used for catching and killing a variety of prey such as small mammals, fish, snakes, and other birds. Talons are a specialty of these raptors, or birds that capture their prey alive.

Most water birds have webs between their toes which function as do "flippers" used by scuba divers. Diving ducks, loons, and grebes, for example, can catch fish under water or pull up the wild celery growing on the bottom of Chesapeake Bay. With an airtight, waterproof coat of feathers, these birds swim with the greatest of ease, insulated against the icy wind and water, or summer heat.

This combination of webbed feet and waterproof covering is characteristic of many kinds of water birds, but there are still other special combinations among the 8600 different bird species that enable birds to survive wherever food and shelter are available.

The ability of some birds to dive and swim, the great skill with which others capture their prey, and their fantastic powers of flight are examples of the adaptations which enable birds to master their environments. There are still other examples; for instance, the efficiency of a bird's digestive system.

The normal temperature of the human body is 98.6°. If a person's temperature rises much above that, he is in serious trouble. But the normal temperature of most birds is well over 100°.

If one considers the amount of energy required to fly across a vast expanse of open sea, or to withstand icy Arctic winds, or to provide a sudden burst of speed in escaping a predator, it is obvious that birds must burn up a great deal of fuel to furnish quick energy and lots of it. To provide this energy, birds must feed on a diet very high in food value and must digest their food rapidly and thoroughly.

A pheasant, feeding in a grainfield, may gobble up a handful of corn in a few minutes and then fly back to the relative safety of the big cattail marsh or heavy brush to digest it. The bird is equipped with a food "storage bin" in its neck called a *crop*. The food moves from this pouch in the neck into the bird's gizzard. The gizzard is a sack filled with sand and gravel which act as grinders.

It has an extremely tough lining and is powered by some of the strongest muscles in the animal kingdom. Since birds have no teeth, the grinding action in the gizzard is a substitute for chewing.

After the gizzard has ground the food to a pulp, it goes into the stomach where it is digested and changed into solutions of sugar and protein that supply the bird with fuel as well as body-building materials.

As is true of airplanes, the size and shape of the wings determine a bird's capacity for speed and maneuverability.

The huge white albatross, celebrated in Coleridge's *Rhyme of the Ancient Mariner,* is truly king of the ocean winds. On wings, with a wingspread up to 11 feet long and but a few inches wide, tapered and perfectly designed to take advantage of the updraft from the waves, an albatross is the world's champion glider. Its wings are

A sooty albatross uses its great wing span to ride the ocean breeze.

not made for flapping flight, however, so when there is no breeze, it is practically "grounded." When there is a breeze, an albatross can easily keep abreast of fast ocean liners for hours on end with hardly a movement of its wings. The sooty and the wandering albatross, can literally go "around the world in eighty days," and records of banded birds show that they often do just that.

Because they are so dependent on ocean winds, the various kinds of albatrosses are concentrated in the southern seas between the Tropic of Capricorn and the Antarctic Circle. In this region, a belt of high winds blows continuously from west to east. On the other hand, the windless doldrums at the equator, stretching across both the Atlantic and the Pacific, are as confining to an albatross as stone walls. Few of the great gliders succeed in crossing these windless areas.

There is another type of bird that differs from the albatross in every way: in size of wing, shape, color, and maneuverability. Yet the hummingbird is an even greater aerialist. The hummingbird family contains not only the best fliers but the smallest and some of the most colorful birds in the world.

A unique wing structure enables the hummingbird to fly by vibrating its wings horizontally (turning them upside down with every forward and backward movement) and to change its speed from about 54 wingbeats per second, while hovering in helicopter fashion, to 200 beats per second while diving and courting. A hummingbird can fly backward, sideways, or in any other direction with ease.

By using ultra high-speed cameras and detailed studies of the feathers, bones, and wing muscles, scientists have been able to analyze the flight of the hummingbird. A ball-and-socket joint, which allows the wing much greater freedom of movement than the similar joint in humans, is one feature. The hummingbird's breast muscles, although tiny, are many times larger in proportion to the wing surface than is true for any other bird.

In addition to the most versatile wings in the world, hummingbirds possess long, needlelike beaks and tongues. With their beaks, they extract nectar and insects

A hummingbird can fly backward, sideways, or in any direction with ease.

It can even hover in one spot in helicopter fashion.

from deep within tubular flower parts. In some species, the bird's bill alone is much longer than its head and body put together. If a person's lips were about 7 feet away from his throat, and his tongue could extend 3 feet beyond that, the proportions would be about the same as they are for a hummingbird.

The combined weight of a dozen Cuban bee hummingbirds would scarcely equal one ounce. At the other end of the scale is the African ostrich. This bird weighs over 300 pounds, stands about 5 feet high at the back, and can stretch its neck to a height of 7 feet.

Ostriches, like penguins, and a few other bird families, cannot fly. But they can run as fast as 40 miles per hour and are extremely wary, intelligent birds. In their native African grasslands, ostriches commonly range with zebras and other big mammals. The big grazing animals

The African ostrich stands about five feet tall at the back, and can stretch its neck to a height of seven feet.

probably scare up insects, small reptiles, and mammals, which are caught by the ostrich. This food rounds out the ostrich's diet of fruit, seeds, and vegetation. In return, the sharp eyes of the towering ostriches can observe danger from a distance. There is no truth to the stories that ostriches bury their heads in the sand when frightened. Instead, they are often the first to give warning of approaching danger.

In summary, feathers are the one common feature possessed by all birds. Otherwise, the variation in birds' beaks, feet, body size, and flying ability is tremendous. It is this wide range of special equipment that accounts for the spread of birds around the world. Birds occupy every type of landscape except the extreme polar ice caps. On rugged mountainsides, in the great deserts, on the oceans, in the forests, in the tropics, or on the barren Arctic tundra, some kind of feathered creature can be found. In each place, the native bird is able to find food, to escape enemies, and to withstand any extremes of the climate. But the same highly specialized equipment that enables a bird to survive may make it dependent on one kind of food or a single habitat type. Slight changes in the environment of such highly specialized birds can spell disaster.

For example, the Everglades kite eats nothing but a single kind of fresh-water snail, *Pomacea.* What happened to the kite when people drained the vast marshes of the Florida Everglades? Elimination of most of the snails was a natural effect of drainage. Following this, the Everglades kite population declined until, by the 1960s, the species faced extinction. Current efforts to restore parts of the Everglades may or may not come in time to save the kites.

The wreck of the *Torrey Canyon* on the southern coast of England in 1967 and the many accidental oil spills in the Gulf of Mexico, Florida, and California have made people in England and America aware that oil destroys the waterproof plumage of birds. Unable to swim or dive, oil-soaked water birds are helpless. Thousands of seagulls, terns, ducks, loons, and grebes have died when their feathers became saturated. Oil destroys the feathers' capacity to insulate the bird against cold air or water. In addition, oil and its by-products destroy both the vegetable and animal life in lakes, rivers, and oceans.

To prevent these disastrous environmental changes, people need to know more about birds, more about their special equipment, and their special requirements. People need to keep in mind that an environment that cannot support birds cannot support people either.

Oil spills at sea spell disaster for water birds when their feathers become saturated.

Migration

chapter four

Many species of birds migrate every fall and spring. Early man tried to explain the mystery of their disappearance with different theories. Swallows were thought to spend the winter hibernating in holes in the ground. Some writers said birds flew up to the moon, arriving there in 60 days. Others were convinced that birds hid in the mud or under water in lakes and streambeds. Even today, many questions regarding migration still remain unanswered. Now people know where and when birds go, but exactly why and how they migrate as they do, no one knows.

Where do the birds go? By what route? How fast do they travel? How long do they live?

In the last half century, the answers to these questions for some of the 8600 species of birds have gradually accumulated. The answers came largely through the practice of banding and marking birds in various ways.

Many birds are banded when in the fledgling stage. There are several methods of capturing birds for banding, such as climbing trees or cliffs and banding the young when the parent birds are off the nest; catching birds on the ground in lightweight nets, called mist nets, and banding and releasing them quickly; or, as in the case of ducks and geese when in the flightless stage, driving them into a large net or enclosed penned area.

Adult birds are often banded in the same ways as the young. Banding is done by trained ornithologists or other wildlife personnel who sometimes train amateurs to help on these important projects.

A nestling hawk receives an identification bracelet so that scientists can trace its later movements and its life history.

In North America, most leg bands are made of aluminum or plastic material. Each has a number and a short message advising the finder to notify the U.S. Fish & Wildlife Service as to the date and place where he found the bird. When a bird is banded, a record is kept of the band—number, species, sex, age, and the date and location where the bird is released. When a banded bird is trapped by an ornithologist, or shot by a hunter, or found dead from any cause, if the person recovering the band notifies the U.S. Fish & Wildlife Service, the complete story of by whom, when, and where the bird was banded is forwarded to him.

This procedure is handled by the Bird Banding Laboratory of the Bureau of Sport Fisheries and Wildlife at Laurel, Maryland. There, records of over 14 million banded birds are kept. Letters pour in by the hundreds every week, reporting the recovery of birds wearing aluminum bracelets.

This is a magnified view of an identification band used by American ornithologists.

Several years ago, a Soviet official delivered a letter to the United States Bureau of Sport Fisheries and Wildlife. The letter, from the Soviet Central Bureau of Bird Ringing (banding), contained complete information on twenty-six birds that had been banded in America and recovered in Russia.

The partridge, pheasant, and quail families do not migrate. These birds usually spend their entire lives within an area of a few acres. In forests of the northern United States, the midnight silence is broken as horned owls hoot amid winter snows and sub-zero temperatures. At the same time, yellow warblers that nested in the same forest as the owl that summer are spending the winter in South America.

In North America, as in Europe, the fall migration is generally from north to south or from colder to warmer climes. But some migrants in North America also fly diagonally eastward from the northwest region, turning south along the Atlantic Coast.

The shore-bird family includes the sandpipers and the plovers, many of which nest in North America but leave the continent and winter in South America. To cite an extreme example, golden plovers nest on the tundra of Alaska and Canada. They then fly to the North Atlantic Coast, follow the ocean south through the Antilles, then fly overland to winter in Brazil and Argentina. In the spring, the same plovers return to the tundra by way of Central America, the Gulf of Mexico, and up the Mississippi Valley, a complete round trip of about 20,000 miles.

Another shore bird, the ruddy turnstone, nests near the North Pole. From the Arctic, the turnstones follow different routes to different continents. Those from the eastern Canadian Arctic and Greenland winter along the English Channel and even farther south. An adult female, banded on her nest on Ellesmere Island, Canada, was shot in Portugal. Another turnstone, banded in England, was collected on her nest on Ellesmere Island. Other groups of turnstones follow the Pacific Coast to Australia; still others take an Atlantic route to South America.

Although the legend persists, white storks have never delivered human babies. Since Biblical times, however, knowledge of the storks' long migration flights, from Europe south to Africa, has been widespread. Recently, banding has allowed scientists to trace the storks' various routes more precisely. From rooftop nests in Germany, Poland, and eastward, the stork population divides into two main groups for the trip south. The western population migrates down across Spain to Gibraltar and then across into Africa. The eastern population swings around the eastern end of the Mediterranean Sea, then southward into Egypt. A smaller group of storks follows the Italian boot south to Sicily and then "hops" across the Mediterranean to North Africa.

The distances traveled by different bird species vary widely. The ruffed grouse in Connecticut may never leave that area, while the woodpeckers that spend the winter there nest somewhat farther north in the summer. If the birds wanted to, they seemingly could move south and spend the winter completely free of Connecticut's sub-zero blizzards and ice storms which temporarily seal off their food supply. But, for reasons no one knows, these birds do not.

Mallards and Canada geese have still another migration pattern—going as far south as necessary to find food and drink and no farther. The United States government and several northern states have deliberately supplied food and water on game-management areas in the north. In response, the flat-faced, web-footed birds have given up their ancestral wintering grounds in Louisiana, Texas, and along the Gulf of Mexico and now spend their winters in areas farther north.

As the environment changed, the migration habits of Canada geese changed with it.

The pintail, the second most abundant duck in North America, is a more impressive traveler. One pintail was found in England only eighteen days after it left Labrador, Newfoundland. A large segment of Manitoba pintails head for the Gulf of Mexico at the first sign of frost on the northern prairies.

What determines the time when birds start from Lake Erie or Lake Baikal and head for South America or North Africa? No one reason supplies all the answers.

In the Midwest, great flocks of insect-eating swallows suddenly leave their summer range while swarms of insects are still available. Obviously, they are not influenced by lack of food. Even stranger, in spring, swallows may return too soon. While snowflakes were still flying along the southwestern shore of Lake Erie, returning tree swallows and barn swallows have been known to starve to death in considerable numbers. It is as though the birds were pulled there by invisible wires, with no force or instinct to make the birds turn back south, only a hundred miles or so, where food and warmth could have easily been found.

Research has shown that, as the days grow longer in the spring, the increased sunlight triggers the release of chemical compounds called hormones into the bloodstream of birds. Like magic potions in some birds, these cause certain glands, the gonads, to enlarge; this is the signal for the birds to gradually shed drab winter plumage in exchange for bright breeding plumage. Also, in some birds, it awakens the overpowering urge to begin the long trek back to the nesting grounds.

Longer days bring about similar changes in the body chemistry of nonmigrating birds such as grouse and wild turkeys, that also put on breeding plumage. The males puff up their feathers, spread their tails into gorgeous fans, and strut before the females. But these birds do not think of flying off to the far north. They go about their lovemaking on the same grounds their ancestors have used for 10,000 years.

How do birds find their way across vast oceans? How can young birds start migratory flights before the older birds with no one to teach them the landmarks along the route?

A Manx shearwater, taken from its nest on the coast of Wales, was released in Boston, Massachusetts. In less than thirteen days, the bird was back at its nest 3200 miles away. This means it spent no time in random searching. It made a direct flight "home" across an ocean with no landmarks along a route where the bird had never flown before. The shearwater must have used some clues from the environment. Was it the sun? the moon? or the stars? at present, no one knows.

A purple martin was taken 234 miles from its house in northern Michigan and released in the dead of night. It was back in its nest the next morning—8 hours and 35 minutes later. How did it know in which direction to go?

When birds present baffling mysteries, scientists respond by devising ingenious ways to solve them. At night, for example, a radar screen can trace birds that otherwise could not be seen and indicate the location, speed, altitude, and size of a flock.

Dr. Franz Sauer, of Hamburg, Germany, went so far as to turn loose some Old World warblers (a highly migratory, night-traveling species) inside the famous Hamburg Planetarium. Under an artificial sky that duplicated the night sky over Siberia, the released birds immediately flew west in the direction that Hamburg would be from Siberia. When the artificial stars were arranged as they would appear over Chicago, the birds flew east without hesitation, again in the direction of Hamburg.

From this evidence, one can conclude that some birds which migrate at night navigate by using celestial bodies as reference points.

Some birds migrate only by day, probably following landmarks that they have learned to recognize by traveling the same route in the company of older birds. At present, no one knows how all the various species find their way.

Another highly useful scientific instrument is a tiny transmitter that emits a "beep" which can be picked up on receiver sets. The transmitter is usually attached to a collar around the bird's neck, which does not interfere with its flight. In this way, it is possible to trace the movements of birds and other animals that otherwise could not be seen.

Much that man needs to know about birds requires no planetariums or electronic equipment. A good set of eyes, ears, binoculars, notebooks, scales, and curiosity can provide fun and knowledge about birds.

As Dr. Ernst Mayr, Director of the Museum of Comparative Zoology, Cambridge, Massachusetts, has said, "If man would save birdlife from himself, for himself, then, of course, he must know the ways and needs of birds."

When wondering about how birds migrate, human beings are influenced by the ways man has found to navigate to faraway places. Man has used the sun, landmarks, the stars, or the magnetic compass, or a combination of all of these to guide him to where he wanted to go. Do birds use these same methods to guide their migrations and to fly safely through natural and man-made hazards? Many scientists have been researching all of these possibilities to find the answer. No matter how many scientists or amateur bird observers are involved in the search, one definite, simple answer will not be found. It is not certain that man will ever fully solve the complex mysteries of migration.

Birds and Pest Control

chapter five

What is a pest? The answer is not simple. Any plant, insect, or other animal that grows where people do not want it to grow, eats what people eat, or causes people discomfort, may be considered a pest that people want to eliminate.

Still, it is unwise to class any plant or animal as completely good or bad. All too often, the same individual may fall into both categories.

In Canada, for example, a farmer smiles when a bobolink sings from his hayfield. During its nesting season, this songster is helpful to the farmer because it eats mostly insects. But in the southeastern United States where the bobolink is seen only as it migrates to and from Argentina, the same bird does not sing, and is such an avid rice eater it is known there only as the "rice bird."

In the days when rice was a major crop in the Carolinas, bobolinks were a serious pest because they ate the sprouting grain in spring and the maturing grain in the fall. This bird, that was helpful to the northern haymaker, was a pest that was killed by the thousands in southern rice fields.

As it left South Carolina, the bobolink stopped in

Jamaica. There the people saw it in still another role. This time as a food provider. Because bobolinks are so fat during their fall migration, roasted bobolinks are still called "butter birds" by Jamaicans. The butter bird, then, is a fine example of how any species, plant or animal, can be considered a friend under certain circumstances and an enemy under others.

This must be kept in mind when discussing pest control. If people eliminate a pest, what takes its place? Does the "pest" at times perform a useful service for which a substitute would then have to be found? Scientists now feel certain that many birds, formerly considered neutral in the fight against insects, weeds, mice, and rats, are really powerful allies.

Owls kill an astounding number of mice and rats.

The raptors—those birds with hooked beaks and sharp talons—were all classed as harmful "pests" by early settlers in North America. The reason was simple enough. These birds killed chickens, rabbits, partridges, and fish. That made them villains in the eyes of hungry human beings.

At the same time, the pioneers worked long and hard to protect their precious grain from mice, rats, chipmunks, squirrels, and blackbirds. Perhaps the settlers were too busy to notice that such raptors as hawks and owls spent most of their time killing and eating those very same grain eaters.

People generally have a favorable image of the bobwhite quail, the pheasant, and the grouse. In winter, these gallinaceous (chickenlike) birds occasionally run short of food. Then they compete with each other for last summer's ragweed seeds, waste corn, and wheat. They also compete with hordes of hungry field mice, sparrows, and starlings that are trying to eat the same food. But who eats mice, sparrows, and starlings? Those same hawks and owls. The raptors are thus performing a valuable service for the pheasants.

Raptors are, however, equally willing to eat quail or pheasant, if these are available. They simply eat whatever is most abundant and easiest to catch. In areas where the game and songbirds have plenty of escape cover near food, the birds are so difficult to catch that hawks and owls turn their attention to mice.

Vast quantities of weed seeds are also eaten by birds. This is of immense value to farmers and helps to reduce the cost of breakfast cereal. Berries of plants injurious to human health, such as poison ivy and poison sumac, are relished by several kinds of birds. Birds' most widely recognized benefit to mankind, however, is their control of insects.

Swallows and nighthawks sweep insects out of the air. Parent wrens make innumerable trips carrying insects to their young. If one watched a tree with woodpeckers, nuthatches, and creepers inspecting the bark, and warblers and vireos searching the leaves for insects and their eggs, then one would know that birds consume a lot of bugs.

How many ounces of insects does a thrush feed her nestlings? Is there any way to measure this? German scientists borrowed an idea from Japanese fishermen and

A thrush feeds its nestlings an enormous number of insects.

their trained cormorants. The scientists put rings around the throats of thrush nestlings to prevent them from swallowing the food their parents brought. They did not leave the rings on long enough to hurt the young birds, just long enough to learn what kinds and how many insects and worms they received.

In this way, the scientists examined more than 50,000 samples of food from more than 12,000 nestlings. They learned that insect-eating birds feed chiefly on species of insects harmful to man and relatively little on beneficial species, such as ladybug beetles.

When one acre of grain is covered with a wire screen that lets insects in but keeps birds out, it is possible to compare the grain produced in the covered plot with another acre that has no screen. This indicates how much grain the birds saved from the insects.

In northern Maine, in 1949 and 1950, foresters studied the number of spruce budworms that birds devoured on 40 acres of infested spruce fir forest. They removed as many birds as they could. They found that warblers had eaten far the greatest number of budworms with thrushes and sparrows eating the next largest amounts. Wandering flocks of cedar waxwings and purple finches also fed heavily on budworms.

Birds apparently consumed 100 to 300 budworm larvae per tree. On another infested 40-acre plot where no birds were removed and their population remained normal, the budworms declined much faster than in the study plot from which birds had been removed. This gave measurable evidence of the role of birds in controlling a forest insect pest.

European foresters have discovered that birdhouses attract certain birds that help to save the trees from various insect enemies. The well-planned use of birdhouses has also been successful in America. Such insectivorous birds as purple martins, tree swallows, house wrens, bluebirds, and prothonotary warblers will readily move into birdhouses and, in turn, they will reduce the insects in the surrounding environment.

In 1847, after two years of hard travel, the Mormon pioneers reached Great Salt Lake in Utah and decided to settle there. Land was cleared, and grain was sown to feed the hardy settlers. The grain was growing nicely when suddenly hordes of grasshoppers invaded the area. If the grain was lost, the Mormon settlers would face starvation.

A monument to California gulls stands in Salt Lake City, Utah.

Then, a lone California gull appeared on the scene, and soon the sky was full of gulls. By feasting on the grasshoppers, the gulls made it possible for the pioneers to feast on grain. The grateful Mormons eventually erected a monument to the gulls. It stands today in Temple Square, Salt Lake City, Utah.

Such a spectacular effect on insects, however, is the exception rather than the rule. At Great Salt Lake, the new grain offered an unusual food source for the insects, attracting them in great swarms. This concentration of grasshoppers was unusual and resulted in an unusual concentration of California gulls that did a very dramatic job of saving the crop.

People who study birds and insects are aware that birds help *regulate* insect populations, but complete *eradication* of insects is possible only in special cases. Birds simply are not abundant enough to control insects in widespread outbreaks that may cover an entire state or more. They are, however, very important factors in regulating insect pests.

If an insect is not killed by a bird, it is likely to be brought down by a dragon fly; by a parasite that kills insects; by a predator such as a bat, a shrew, a fish; by unfavorable weather; or by some other factor. All of these operate to keep insect populations within bounds. Factors such as these not only keep the numbers of insects in check, but also operate on mice, birds and even plants. All these factors interact to keep the community of living things stable.

Under normal conditions, when one kind of the many

members of a plant and animal community becomes overabundant, something happens that reduces its numbers and restores balance. Thousands of so-called pests—weeds, insects, mice—exist in fields, orchards, and forests. Most of them are unnoticed by people because their populations are not large enough to be conspicuous or to cause a lot of damage.

A stable community with these built-in control factors contrasts sharply with a monoculture. A monoculture is created when a single species of plant such as corn or wheat is grown by farmers in a huge block covering several square miles. These abnormal concentrations of a single plant naturally attract abnormal concentrations of insects and outbreaks of plant diseases beyond the control of normal bird populations. Because there are no built-in controls in a monoculture, farmers turn to chemical pesticides.

Monoculture farming has been spreading across the American Great Plains. One cannot blame the farmer who has been encouraged to adopt monoculture instead of diversified farming. The incentive to produce the maximum amount of grain per acre is overpowering. After all, over half the human race was undernourished by 1970, and the population promises to double again in three decades.

Consequently, when it was discovered during the 1940s that DDT, a complex chemical compound of the elements carbon, hydrogen, and chlorine, would kill insects as if by magic, men hailed the day when their ancient enemies would be completely wiped out.

During World War II, however, an incident occurred

at an experimental rocket base on the coast of New Jersey that should have warned the public that DDT is not an unmixed blessing. Flies were so numerous on the beach that they interfered with the rocket project. Help was called for, and the base was sprayed with DDT, as was the adjacent sea water. Within a few hours, the flies were dead and the rocketeers happily went back to work, impressed with the wonders of this brand-new insecticide. A week later, a mysterious epidemic littered the beach with tons of dead and decaying fish. The stench attracted vast swarms of flies all over again. Thus scientists learned that DDT would kill fish as well as insects.

After the war, ornithologists discovered that DDT has many adverse effects on birds. It can kill them, or cause them to become infertile, or to lay eggs with shells so thin that the embryos cannot develop and hatch.

For example, to dairyman John Briscoe, of Lime Rock, Connecticut, plagued with flies in his barn, DDT appeared to offer a solution. Flies "died like flies" that first summer when DDT was sprayed about the premises. The next summer, however, not all the flies died as readily. Some merely became "groggy" and were eaten by Mr. Briscoe's ducklings in the barnyard. After eating many of these flies, the ducklings became ill and died. This alert farmer suspected the sick flies might be the cause of his sick ducklings. Thereafter, he kept his ducklings away from the barn and had no more trouble.

Mr. Briscoe's experience points up three aspects of DDT:

Unlike other chemical compounds, when DDT is

eaten, most of it is not broken down and is not eliminated from the bodies of most of the eaters. Instead, some of it stays in the tissues of the insect or animal and, as the eater takes in more food containing DDT, more and more of this deadly poison accumulates in its tissues.

DDT can readily kill birds which feed on insects that have concentrated the poison in their bodies but are themselves not killed by it. The DDT stays in the bird's body so that when it eats enough poisoned insects, it dies from the accumulated DDT.

Thirdly, the incredibly rapid rate at which insects reproduce enables them to evolve a new strain which is immune to DDT within a single year. The few flies which DDT could not kill quickly replaced the ones that were killed with offspring that were resistant to man's new weapon.

Added to Mr. Briscoe's experience with DDT and ducklings and the military's experience in New Jersey with DDT and fish is a long list of other poisoning incidents, including that of shrimp, oysters, robins, mourning doves, ospreys, eagles, and many other species that face extinction, seemingly because of DDT.

After the war, manufacture of DDT became a multimillion dollar business. Similar poisons, even more potent than DDT, were invented.

At Clear Lake, California, for example, professional pest controllers decided, in 1949, to rid the 19-mile-long lake of gnats. They carefully applied TDE (DDD), a close relative of DDT and known to be low in toxicity to mammals, at a rate of only fourteen parts of poison to one *billion* parts of lake water. Some years later, in 1957, about 100 birds, western grebes, mysteriously died in one month. At first, TDE was not suspected because the very dilute application was not poisonous to fish-eating birds. However, chemical analyses revealed that somehow the grebes had ingested large amounts of TDE. How Clear Lake water, containing only fourteen parts TDE per billion parts of water, could poison a fish-eating diver bird was at first a mystery.

Further tests disclosed that the entire "food chain" in Clear Lake was contaminated with TDE. The plankton, which are microscopic plants and animals, made up the first link in the food chain. These creatures had filtered the poison from the water until, in proportion, TDE was 265 times as concentrated in their bodies as it was in the water of the lake. Small fish feeding on the plankton carried 500 times as much poison in their bodies as there was in the water. In turn, the fish-eating grebes had about 80,000 times the concentration of poison in their bodies—enough to kill them. Even the cooked parts of the popular game fish from Clear Lake had a far higher level of TDE than is allowed in domestic meat by the U.S. Food & Drug Administration.

In 1971, more than 20 years after the lake was carefully treated by experts, the TDE was still present and the grebes' ability to reproduce was seriously threatened.

Many other lakes around the world now display the same concentrating effect of DDT and similar pesticides. These poisons need not be deliberately added to water to create the problems. Farmlands, forests, orchards, marshes, or other land areas are often deliberately poisoned, to try to control pests. From these areas, the poisons wash into smaller streams, which flow on into rivers and lakes, and finally into the oceans.

British investigators have found that the eggs of fish-eating cormorants contain twenty-six times as much pesticide as the eggs of kittiwakes which eat plankton instead of fish. A fish eater is higher up on the food chain than a plankton feeder; therefore, it takes in a much higher conentration of DDT in its diet.

A parallel situation exists in the case of raptors that feed on birds that depend on insects. Many insects, as well as earthworms, can concentrate DDT in their bodies. When poisoned worms and insects are eaten in quantities by robins, for example, the songbird receives a lethal dose. The sharp-shinned hawk that eats myrtle warblers that have fed on thousands of insects loaded with DDT, will suffer the same fate as the western grebe of Clear Lake.

On the positive side, insecticides have reduced the numbers of malaria-carrying mosquitoes, thus saving untold numbers of human lives from this dread disease. Today, the human race occupies every habitable section of the globe and is still cramped for space. Any attempt to open new land areas that are unavailable due to insect competition is welcomed by the World Health Organization.

In the early 1950s, Dr. Rachel L. Carson, a scientist employed by the U.S. Department of the Interior, began to question whether DDT, as an insecticide, was worth its cost in other forms of animal life. Her book, *Silent Spring*, focused world-wide attention on the question.

While the subject is still being debated by the champions and the opponents of chlorinated hydrocarbons, the search goes on for alternatives: selective insecticides that will control the target species and yet not wipe out man's natural allies such as beneficial insects, birds, and mammals.

Furthermore, if people would apply what they have learned about good range management, soil and water management, and forest ecology, the insect competitors would have a much harder time of it.

A case in point is the great caterpillar war fought in New Mexico in 1970 and 1971. On one side were cattlemen about to spray a DDT-like pesticide, toxaphene, on the grass-eating range moth. On the other side were people concerned about the effects of the poison on their local drinking water and on fish. Also, if spraying was used, the natural enemies of the range moth would be affected: camel crickets, ground beetles, ants, robber flies, birds, mice, badgers, coyotes, and skunks. The environment for many would be drastically changed.

A known fact of good range management is that if the land had not been overgrazed by too many cattle in the first place, the nutritious native grasses would not have been wiped out and replaced by blue grama grass. Blue grama grass is a favorite food of the range moth. The moths were never able to seriously damage the native grasses, but once those were overgrazed, it was easy for the range moth to feed on the blue grama grass and to increase their numbers steadily. The real enemy of the range and the ally of the range moth is overgrazing by too many cattle per square mile.

The cattlemen won that battle, and the spray was

used. But more and more today, concerned citizens are demanding that good preventive management practices be used, rather than introducing more poisons into the environment.

In England, there is a hopeful turn of events. Realizing that perfect, unblemished apples represent previous spraying with DDT, the English housewife is often willing to pay more for fruit and vegetables that show a little bit of insect damage. This way she knows she is not absorbing an insecticide along with her food.

If people would be willing to accept an ear of corn with a few kernels missing because an insect got there first, or an apple with a blemish that affects only a small portion of the fruit, then grocery bills would eventually go down instead of up.

In summary, according to the World Health Organization, a few million people around the globe probably owe their lives to chlorinated hydrocarbons. At the same time, these compounds have spread throughout the air, water, and lands of the entire globe and are known to persist for many years, resulting in the death of many birds, beneficial insects, and microscopic plants and animals on which mankind depends.

The search for compounds that will decompose rapidly and kill only one specific pest continues. Meanwhile, although the exploding human population can spare less and less food for other animals, people would do well to try to restore a diversified landscape on both farm and forest land. This would make the environment of both birds and people far less dangerous and far more interesting.

Carrying Capacity

chapter six

About 50 years ago, a well-meaning Ohio legislature designated Ohio's favorite gamebird, the bobwhite quail, a songbird. This meant that the quail could not be hunted because songbirds are protected by law. The law makers reasoned that if one quail hen produces a dozen baby quail, a thousand hens will produce 12,000 downy chicks. Proponents of the bill argued that complete protection from hunting for a few years would bring about a rapid increase in this very popular bird.

Support for the bill came from ardent hunters who wanted to see their favorite quarry become abundant to assure the bird's future, which would then provide them good hunting in later years. Support also came from farmers who valued the bird because it feeds on insects and weed seeds. Bird watchers and artists were fond of the attractive bobwhite quail. Without a doubt, a spectacular increase in the population of bobwhite would be welcomed by all.

In the neighboring state, Indiana, the Hoosier hunters continued to hunt their quail. Many Ohio hunters went to Indiana to join in the sport. Others said they were content to wait until Ohio's quail flock increased.

Twenty years went by and everyone was still waiting for the big increase in quail. In some years, the quail population was even lower than before the quail bill was passed. In other years, the birds were more abundant. Biologists in Ohio and Indiana began to compare notes. Curiously enough, they found that the bobwhite populations decreased and increased during the same years and at the same rate in both states. After 20 years of complete protection in Ohio, the birds were no more numerous there than in Indiana where they had been steadily hunted. Over in Illinois, just west of Indiana, the quail were consistently more abundant than in Ohio, although Illinois quail hunters numbered about 600,000 per year.

In some states the bobwhite quail is a protected songbird; in others it is a highly prized game bird.

Hunters in Ohio blamed the foxes, hawks, and owls for keeping down the quail population. Biologists, however, pointed out that there were more of these quail eaters per square mile in Illinois than in Ohio. Many hunters refused to believe the scientists, and there was much heated debate throughout the state. In the midst of the controversy, the wildlife biologists around the country continued their studies of quail, pheasants, grouse, and other birds.

In Thomasville, Georgia, Dr. Herbert L. Stoddard finished an exhaustive study of the bobwhite which had taken him several years to complete. He learned what kinds of plants and insects furnished the quails' food, what plants furnished nesting material, what type of hiding places furnished cover from enemies. The numbers of dead quail, those eaten by different predators, those dying from various diseases, or those killed in sudden rainstorms, were carefully recorded.

In Ohio and other northern states, similar studies were in progress. In New England, deep snow, ice storms, and bitter cold added new hazards to those Dr. Stoddard had recorded in Georgia. Otherwise, the quail populations in both parts of the country faced similar kinds of dangers.

Painstaking research was gradually building a backlog of new facts about the lives and times of these birds. Students of quail biology could not find the answers in books because such books had yet to be writen. They could not ask the hunters because the hunters did not know, nor did the farmers, the bird watchers, and the artists. If they wanted to know what a quail ate, the biologists had to find out from the quail, just as Dr. Stoddard had done in Georgia. And so, examination of several thousand quail crops and gizzards gave the biologists information on what quail like to eat.

In the same way, examination of the foods eaten by foxes, hawks, and owls would tell how many quail the predators ate at various times of the year. Examination of quail found dead in the fields showed whether they died of disease, starvation, freezing, or drowning. Checking with thousands of hunters year after year gave clues to the number of quail that hunters took.

In a hidden nest, quail chicks are hatched. They leave the nest as soon as their down feathers are dry.

Still it came as something of a surprise to discover that no matter what part of the country the quail occupied, about three-fourths of those alive in the fall died from some cause before the following spring. The causes of death might vary from one place to another, but in general, the end results were about the same whether birds were hunted or not.

This is not to say that when there is a density of one bobwhite on every two acres of land in Georgia there will be a similar density in Wisconsin. Near the Canadian border, deep snows often bury the weed seeds and grain, which quail eat in winter, for days on end. A quail cannot live for many hours without adequate food. Therefore, except in a series of mild winters, quail will never be very abundant in Wisconsin or northern Ohio and probably never as abundant as in Georgia.

This was why the expected increase of quail in Ohio never happened. Yet in all parts of the country the same holds true: for every four quail alive in the fall, only one remains in the spring.

Although deep snow and bitter cold can limit the population of quail on the northern edge of their range, winter holds no terrors for the ruffed grouse. This northern cousin of the quail has withstood thousands of blizzards. But, for reasons as yet unexplained, grouse are not found farther south. Thus the carrying capacity, the number of animals an area can support, for ruffed grouse in southern North America is zero, quite the opposite of the bobwhite.

Climate is not the only factor that determines carrying

capacity, whether birds will live or die, or how many and what kinds can survive in any given area. The ring-necked pheasant, for example, is more abundant on soil underlain by limestone rather than sandstone because the calcium in limestone is important in their diet. Thus calcium also affects carrying capacity.

An area of fertile soil carries more birds and other animal life than one that is infertile. But even on the most fertile soils, when the ground is plowed under right up to fence lines, when hedgerows and wood lots are destroyed, or when the land is occupied by buildings and roads, very little if any food or cover for wildlife can grow on it. Its carrying capacity for birds will be reduced to practically zero. Land use affects carrying capacity.

In some instances, food and shelter are accidentally made available. Even in large cities, for example, house sparrows, starlings, and domestic pigeons can scavenge for food in the streets and find shelter under the eaves. City parks, which contain trees, shrubs, grass and flowers, and water, may offer birds nesting materials, some insect life, and even food provided by people. In that case, the park definitely increases the carrying capacity of the city for some birds.

In northern Europe, rooftops built by people for people accidentally provided ideal nesting sites for the white storks.

In any case, these man-made benefits to birds, whether accidental or intentional, cannot benefit a species which is too "wild" to overcome its fear of being close to people.

No city park is going to contain a wild eagle or prairie chicken for very long, even if food and nesting sites are available. The behavior of individual birds also affects the carrying capacity of any environment.

Still another factor that determines bird density is the degree of crowding which a species will tolerate. On 1800 acres of good range in Minnesota, biologist Ralph T. King studied the ruffed grouse for seven years. He learned that no matter how many of these birds were present in the fall, when it was time for the males to strut and drum (the courtship ritual) in the spring, there was

In northern Europe, rooftops provide shelter for people and also serve as nesting sites for white storks.

only one bird, male or female, for every four acres. The October populations in Mr. King's study area varied from less than 500 birds to 1000, but regardless of that, the population in spring for seven years in a row was about 450 birds. Mr. King concluded that each bird required four acres of "elbow room" in spring or eight acres per breeding pair. In other words, each spring, on Minnesota's ruffed grouse range, the birds spread themselves out. Each male drums, fights other males, and defends his mate and his own territory of about eight acres. The carrying capacity of that particular range is, therefore, one ruffed grouse to every four acres, or 160 birds per square mile.

Birds will not tolerate overcrowding. Their courtship behavior and territorial defense very effectively prevent any surplus birds from nesting. The weaker birds are thus kept from reproducing so that only the strongest birds survive.

The carrying capacity of any land or water area may change for better or worse in terms of the welfare of various birds and mammals. Some favorite ruffed grouse foods, for example, are aspen buds, apple buds, wild rose seeds, and wintergreen berries. As a forest grows older and the shade becomes darker, many of these plants will disappear because of the decrease in sunlight. When this happens, lack of food will then reduce the carrying capacity for grouse. At the same time the carrying capacity for birds which do well in mature forests will increase.

How the land is used really determines what kinds of

plants can grow on it, and plants, in turn, determine how many and what kinds of birds and mammals can live on it. Even those birds that eat only fish depend indirectly on plants, because the fish feed either on plants or on other plant-eating fish.

The seed-eating bird obviously depends on plants, although its offspring may eat only insects for the first few days of its life. The insects, in turn, like the fish, either feed directly on plants or on other insects which eat plants.

Plant life depends on a combination of sunlight, certain elements in the air, and minerals in the soil and water. It is the primary food, or the foundation, on which all life depends. Plant life also provides the oxygen that animals, including human beings, breathe.

No single factor, be it food, temperature, precipitation, or predators, determines the carrying capacity of a given area by itself. Each factor in the environment operates in combination with the others. They are dependent on one another and constantly interact. When one factor is changed, such as the amount of sunlight on the forest floor, all the factors must change accordingly.

Some of these changes will benefit certain species of birds to the detriment of others. The more mankind knows about the effects of environmental changes, the better chance people will have of maintaining an environment suitable for birds and people.

Food Habits

chapter seven

People usually enjoy eating different kinds of foods. Most of them would object to eating the same kind of food for lunch that they had had for breakfast. This would not apply to the food habits of birds. In fact, some kinds of birds spend their entire lives eating only one kind of food.

The Everglades kite of Florida feeds exclusively on one kind of fresh-water snail called *Pomacea*. This kite, or snail hawk, is equipped with a long, curved upper beak, or mandible, which just fits into the spiraled snail shell and extracts the flesh. Unlike its distant relative, the osprey, this hawk could not catch a fish to save its life. Its life, in fact, depends on this one species of snail that could easily be wiped out by the drainage of the Florida Everglades.

Several species of birds feed almost entirely on flying insects. They might not even recognize as food a dead insect or a live one that was not moving. Such birds include the swifts, many of the swallows, and the nightjars.

Just as the gaping engines of a jet plane sometimes suck in a flock of starlings over an airfield, so the gaping mouths of nightjars scoop up flying insects. Encircling this wide open mouth is a row of strong, rakelike bristles that help the bird to strain gnats and mosquitoes out of the air. As many as 500 mosquitoes have been found in the stomach of a single nightjar.

As the name implies, nightjars hunt and sing at night—some alone, some in flocks. The birds are often called goatsuckers as well as nightjars because years ago the story was spread that these night-flying birds would suckle milk from goats if not driven away from the herds. Even though the story was not true and the birds eat only flying insects, the name has remained.

The gaping mouth of the nightjar serves as a funnel that sucks in flying insects.

The common nightjar, a native of Europe, and the American nighthawks, whippoorwills, and poor-wills are all closely related.

A wide variety of birds feed on fish. The list includes loons, grebes, albatrosses, shearwaters, tropic birds, pelicans, boobies, gannets, cormorants, frigate birds, herons, bitterns, ibises, mergansers, ospreys, eagles, gulls, terns, murres, puffins, and kingfishers. These birds are all so skillful that commerical fishermen are known to watch for flocks of some of them, such as gulls and terns, hovering over a school of fish and thus know where to set their nets.

For over 1400 years, Oriental fishermen have trained cormorants to catch fish for them. By placing a ring around the bird's throat, it is kept from swallowing any but very small fish. A string may be attached to the cormorant to retrieve it, depending on whether it is trained to return on its own. When the feathered diver comes up with a gullet full of fish, it is brought on board a boat where the fishermen immediately force open its bill and make the helper disgorge its catch.

A well-trained cormorant may catch over 100 fish per hour. Because these birds can work until they are about twenty years old, some trained cormorants receive better care than some bird dogs.

Wading birds, such as herons, feed extensively on fish, but usually do not take many warm-water game fish, such as bass, perch, or catfish, because they do their fishing around the shallow margins and cannot wade in deeper waters.

The diving ducks, such as the red-breasted merganser, cause consternation among trout and salmon fishermen when they catch considerable numbers of these prized fish in rivers, lakes, and reservoirs. Where fish are artificially concentrated in hatcheries, the fish ducks, herons, and kingfishers may make serious inroads on the crop before the fish are "planted" in waters open to human fishermen. By and large, however, the total effect of fish-eating birds on commercial and sport fishing is slight.

Fishermen may be jealous of those birds that eat their fish, but certainly no one envies the scavenger birds who clean up dead animals, the dead fish in lakes and along

Sharp-eyed vultures may not be pretty, yet their food habits provide a service mankind could hardly do without.

beaches, the food scraps in garbage, and the waste from commercial fishing or whaling ships. Decaying carcasses of cattle and sheep, wild deer, and elk are seldom around for long because sharp-eyed vultures, eagles, ravens, and crows take over and save people the job of burying them. If it were not for the work of seagulls, eagles, and crows along popular beaches, the stench of rotting fish would drive people away. Not only the dead fish, but bits of hamburgers and picnic remains become food for seaside birds.

On the high seas, there are albatrosses, shearwaters, fulmars, and petrels hard at work. Most of their food consists of aquatic animal life, alive and dead, but they will readily follow ocean-going ships to pick up castoff garbage.

In southern California, crows have learned that drive-in theaters offer them an easy breakfast. In the early morning, flocks of hungry crows arrive to eat popcorn, bits of hot dogs, hamburgers, and other trash carelessly tossed out of cars by movie viewers the night before.

The seed-eating birds are not so easily classified as to their good or bad services to man. People eat corn, wheat, rye, and rice and so do mallards, pheasants, blackbirds, bobolinks, and wild geese. But, in order to raise corn, people have to kill ragweeds, smartweeds, foxtail grass, and pigweeds. The seeds of these weeds are also the favorite foods of the very same birds.

People do not like thistles because of their prickly thorns. Goldfinches eat thistle seeds and kill many a thistle by swallowing the seed before it can sprout. Sparrows, finches, and grosbeaks eat the seeds of many plants which humans consider obnoxious weeds. At the same time, they eat millet, wheat, and other grains that are also food for humans and domestic animals.

Some birds, such as crossbills, eat seeds from the cones of various spruces, firs, and pines, but these trees produce millions of seeds, more than could ever possibly grow into trees, so the birds have little effect on commercial timber production.

Even from such a hasty look at the eating habits of birds, the influence of man can be readily seen. By changing the environment, man may drastically change the food habits of many bird species. Wildlife managers and bird lovers may deliberately alter the birds' food supply, but many other environmental changes are made with no thought about the effect on birds.

For example, some years ago in Great Britain, the English great tit discovered how to open milk bottles and feed on the cream, a practice which, in time, spread. This transfer of fats and carbohydrates from grass to dairy cow to bird was not planned by British bird lovers, yet the milk bottle on the doorstep became an important factor in the environment of the birds.

Along the Atlantic Coast, Maryland and Delaware landowners have converted thousands of acres of forest into cornfields since World War II. The mechanical cornpicker has led to a great saving in man hours of labor, but as it operates, the machine drops a small amount of the corn in the field. This corn has been such a good food supply to migrant Canada geese that the honkers no longer go much farther south in quest of winter food.

The wildlife refuge manager, on the other hand, deliberately plants corn and other grains and leaves the entire crop for the birds. In the northern states, supplying sunflower seeds, millet, and suet for backyard and window sill birdfeeders has become an important part of the groceryman's business.

The question arises, "Is it really helping birds to make them dependent on people for their winter food?" Some people argue that the increased supply of food enables more birds to survive the rigors of winter in New England. Others claim that the chickadees, blue jays, cardinals, and other common winter birds from New York to Maine would be better off if they migrated farther south. They feel the warmer climate would not take the toll of bird mortality that blizzards and deep snows are apt to do.

While there may be no clear-cut answer to this argument, it is interesting to note that a century ago, wild birds, such as ducks, geese, wild turkey, grouse, and doves, to name a few, were an important source of food for people. Feeding birds for pleasure only was a rarity, indeed. In today's environment, partly by accident, partly by intention, people are an important source of food for birds.

Although measuring the exact effect of providing food for birds may be difficult, there seems little doubt that if birds did not eat insects, garbage, dead animals, and weed seeds, the earth would scarcely be a fit place for people.

The American robin helps to control insect populations.

Bird Mortality

chapter eight

To kill a songbird has long been considered an act of foolishness. Nevertheless, each year thousands of birds die or are killed, and are replaced by young birds. Because the total numbers remain fairly stable, the conclusion is that the number of birds born must roughly equal the number that die. This balance will exist until the environment of a particular species of bird undergoes a change to which the bird cannot adapt.

Some bird species on which people depend for food or recreation are disappearing at an alarming rate. People need to know more about what kills them. Obviously, something in the bird's environment has become a serious hazard: The air? Water? Natural enemies? In some cases, the trouble is easy to identify; in others, it baffles investigators.

Consider, for example, ducks and duck hawks (peregrine falcons). Although the falcon can kill the duck with ease, together they have flown the skies of eastern North America for thousands of years. Bald eagles also kill and eat ducks when they have the opportunity. Since World War II, both duck hawks and eagles have almost disappeared from the northeastern United States. With their ancient enemies fading from the scene, it might be expected that ducks would increase noticeably.

Unfortunately, the reverse is true. Many species of ducks are declining, regardless of the raptor decline. In fact, there is no evidence that hawks, owls, or eagles catch enough adult waterfowl to make much difference to the duck supply. But what about ducklings? Or eggs? Significant numbers of duck eggs are, in fact, eaten by hungry crows, skunks, foxes, snakes, and other predators that search the ground for birds' nests. Does this have any real effect on total duck mortality?

Prior to 1940, millions of small ponds, often called potholes, dotted the prairies of the northern United States and southern Canada. Ducks of various kinds nested around the edge of every pothole. During World War II, the United States Department of Agriculture offered to share the cost with any farmer who would drain his wetlands and thus increase productive acres, a practice that continued and accelerated after the war. The result was more wheat and less habitat for ducks.

As the potholes were drained, nesting ducks were forced to seek out nest sites on the remaining wetlands. This concentrated the ducks' nests so that the skunks, snakes, and other predators around the undrained potholes had no difficulty in finding their prey.

Before the farmers drained the prairies, the ducks could easily lay more eggs than the egg eaters could find. Even today, the predators obviously do not find all of the eggs. For the mallards and pintails nesting in southern

Manitoba, however, two changes in their environment have brought about a real change in the relationship between egg layers and egg eaters.

First, the drainage of potholes has reduced the ducks' nesting habitat. Secondly, the raccoon, a very efficient nest finder, has extended its range northward into the birds' nesting grounds. The result is that a great many duck nests are now destroyed by predators. Countering this, in some cases, are man's efforts to reduce the skunk, raccoon, and bull snake populations, efforts which pay dividends in additional ducklings.

The king snake is one of many predators searching for birds' eggs.

On the other hand, many birds are so persistent in their efforts to produce a brood that they will lay a second or third clutch of eggs if their first is destroyed. Destruction of some nests may actually have advantages.

Most mallards start nesting at about the same time; therefore, their eggs all hatch at the same time. During this time, the prairie is perfectly capable of whipping up a rain or hail storm that will kill every duckling just out of the egg. But if some ducklings are already half-grown and others are still within the eggs, sheltered from weather by the mother duck, sudden natural disaster will catch only those that are vulnerable at the time. The predators, in one sense, force the mallards to nest at different times, which is to the duck's advantage.

It is worthwhile to examine the *real* effect of egg losses on total production before deciding whether to try to reduce the number of predators. As a general rule, if the nesting habitat has been damaged very much, predators do not make serious inroads on production of young birds. In special cases, however, they may have a real effect.

Mr. Harold Duebbert, waterfowl biologist working at Jamestown, North Dakota, demonstrated that he can reduce nest losses to very low levels merely by controlling the kind of vegetation on the prairie. A mixture of intermediate wheatgrass, and sweet clover, alfalfa, and certain weeds makes such a tall, dense cover that skunks and other predators do not try to hunt in it. The ducks respond by nesting at the rate of about one nest or more per acre, a density practically unheard of elsewhere.

If waterfowl biologists were permitted to apply this technique over larger areas of the prairie, the future of American waterfowl would be assured. Unfortunately, the world-wide demand for, and the prices paid for, wheat and corn are greater than those paid for mallards. The landowner quite naturally raises the crop that will bring in the most dollars per acre. This economic fact of life has a far-reaching effect on the numbers of birds that live and die throughout the world.

Using mallards and pintails for another example, these ducks are the favorites of duckhunters as well as of bird watchers. The drainage of the prairie potholes and marshes has reduced the ability of the land to produce young ducks. At the same time, drainage and filling of the great marshes along the seashore and river bottoms to the south have reduced the areas where the ducks can safely feed and rest in winter. With less habitat available, the birds are forced to concentrate in whatever habitat remains. This makes the birds easier for hunters, eagles, falcons, and disease germs to find.

Improved autos, roads, and airplanes also make it much easier for hunters to go where the ducks are during the fall and winter. There are now more hunters and fewer ducks than in former days. This means that in some years hunters can kill a greater number of ducks than the number that matured in that year. This is especially true when severe droughts dry up many of the remaining potholes. Consequently, rigid laws governing the number of ducks that each hunter is allowed, and the number of days he can hunt are designed to keep the number of ducks shot equal to, or less than, the number produced in any year. Well-informed hunters who respect the ducks generally support such regulations.

Waterfowl are limited to marshes and river bottoms for their food and resting areas. The hunter whose hiding place is in the favorite haunts of the mallard knows the birds must come to him. In contrast, the pheasant, grouse, or quail hunter must pursue his quarry on foot. As these gallinaceous birds become increasingly scarce, they are increasingly hard to find. The hunting declines as the hunters grow tired and quit, leaving fair numbers of these birds in the bushes. As a mortality factor then, the hunter's gun may actually determine how many ducks will be alive next fall; but hunting's total effect on pheasants or grouse is far from critical.

Guns could kill the last golden eagle or the last bald eagle. It is doubtful, however, if shooting will ever endanger the Wilson's snipe, a small shorebird that is just too difficult to hunt and to shoot. As a bird killer, then, the gun is detrimental to some species, but not to others.

In the great marshes of the western United States and Canada, hunters are not the only hazard confronting water birds. A deadly poison caused by bacteria that can grow only in the absence of air kills aquatic birds by the hundreds of thousands. It is called botulism or western duck sickness. This bacterium *Clostridium botulinum* is divided into six types, A through F, each of which produces a distinct toxin. Types A, B, D, E, and F cause botulism in man and other mammals, but they rarely affect wild birds. As far as scientists can determine, it is type C that affects wild bird populations.

The bird contracts botulism if it happens to be feeding in a marsh where the conditions are right for the bacteria to be active. The bird swallows the toxin made by the bacteria and absorbs it through the lining of the digestive tract. It enters the blood stream, then attacks the nervous system, causing paralysis and death. This poison kills gulls, terns, grebes, and shorebirds as well as ducks, geese, and swans.

Biologists realized that oxygen would prevent the bacteria growth. They took steps to aerate the water, to develop an antitoxin, and to collect sick ducks and to try to save them by forcing pure water down their throats. These measures help considerably, but botulism remains a deadly killer of water birds and is, therefore, a challenge to man.

Fowl cholera is equally serious, not only to wild birds, but to domestic fowl. Very little is known about the cause, spread, and possible treatment of this disease. It is an infection and must enter the tissues of its host to bring about its ill effects. How the infection is introduced into a water fowl population is not known. Scientists do know that overcrowding favors the spread of this contagious disease. The famous Long Island ducklings are occasionally victims of fowl cholera, as are flocks of chickens and turkeys. There is still a great deal of research to be done to eradicate this contagious infection.

The water of some lakes and ponds turns green, especially in late summer. This is caused by countless billions of tiny plants called algae. When algae grow so profusely that the water of the lake appears to be almost the color and consistency of pea soup, the lake is said to be "blooming." Certain strains of algae are referred to as "blue greens," which is a somewhat misleading term because their color varies from black to red and yellow. The color of the Red Sea is apparently due to the red tint given it by one of the blue-green algae that grow there.

Unfortunately, the blue-green algae become deadly poisonous when their growth is abundant. This condition is called algae poisoning, and every bird or mammal that drinks from a lake blooming with blue-green algae usually dies from it in a matter of hours. In 1948, hundreds of dead birds around Fox Lake, Minnesota, alerted farmers to the fact that the lake contained algae poisoning. This was not, however, before large numbers of hogs, ducks, chickens, dogs, and other animals had also been poisoned. In several other poisoning instances, dying birds were the first sign of danger.

Most species of algae are not poisonous and even the blue-greens become deadly only when environmental conditions are right for rapid reproduction. By permitting too much fertilizer, sewage, and detergents to run off into lakes, however, people are literally flirting with death because the next algae bloom resulting from that kind of overnourishment may be blue-green algae. Furthermore, other species of algae can cause death to fish and other aquatic life when the plants are overly abundant. When the plants of such an overgrowth die, the process of decay absorbs so much oxygen from the water that there is not enough remaining to sustain the aquatic animal life. Without oxygen, fish are smothered and literally "drown." This process, known as *eutrophication,* changes the environment of birds and people by robbing lakes of their ability to produce food.

In the fall of 1963, at Eau Claire, Wisconsin, a new thousand-foot television tower represented something new in the environment of birds—something new and deadly. Birds had been flying over what is now the Eau Claire area since prehistoric times. The steel tower that pierced the sky for almost a fifth of a mile was squarely in the migration route of millions of birds. It was a hazard made even more inviting on overcast nights by aircraft warning lights on the tower, which seemed to attract birds.

On September 18, the migrating birds arrived in waves, milling around the lights. They collided with the tower, with each other, with the supporting cables, and with the ground. On the morning of September 19, 5595 dead birds were found around the tower. Forty-two species were among the dead. Magnolia warblers suffered the highest count, 846. Later, the surviving birds either changed flight course, or those with the instinct to follow that path were eliminated.

Such collisions with man-made structures are not new. Completion of the 555-foot-tall Washington monument in 1884 had brought death to thousands of birds. Then few other birds hit the monument until 1931 when aviation beacons were installed—which seemed both to attract and to blind the migrants.

With the steady increase in numbers of towers, some over twice as high as the one at Eau Claire, the need to locate them outside of known heavy bird-migration lanes is obvious. Also, serious attention to the problem of making towers visible to night-migrating birds is a challenge to man's advances in engineering and electronics.

Lights on the Empire State Building in New York City and at Perry's Monument in Put in-Bay, Ohio, are turned off during the peak of the migration periods. With no lights to blind them, or attract them to the obstacle, mortality among birds is reduced.

In a single night these birds were killed when they collided with the Empire State Building in New York City.

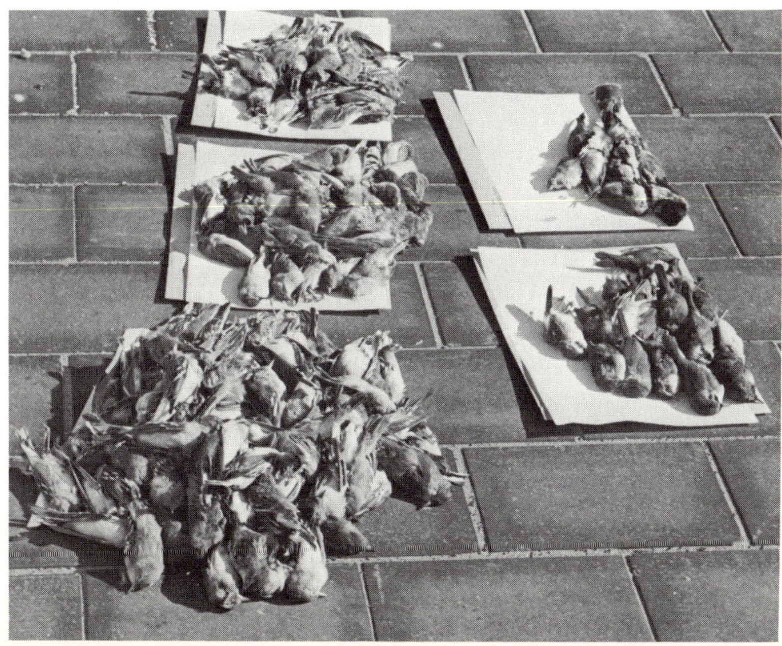

The electric power companies have shown considerable ingenuity in reducing the number of birds electrocuted on wires. Near Aberdeen, Idaho, possibly 100 eagles are electrocuted on transmission lines every year. When an eagle's spread wings simultaneously touch two wires, the circuit is closed. A shower of sparks, flame, and a dead eagle result. This has been corrected elsewhere by putting the lines farther apart, or by erecting special perches which are high enough so that the eagles miss the wires.

Ospreys on Long Island, New York, nesting on top of power poles, occasionally dragged long, wet strands of seaweed across two charged wires. The result was in-

Electric power lines offer both nesting sites and death traps to ospreys.

stant electrocution. A nesting platform placed three or four feet from the side of the power pole was more to the ospreys' liking and solved the problem.

The very fact that collisions and electrocutions are sudden and obvious, however, makes these factors less dangerous and easier to solve than slow subtle changes in the air, soil, and water that cannot be seen and which may last for decades.

Mr. Alexander Sprunt IV and Mr. Frank Ligas, of the National Audubon Society, have conducted a continental survey of bald eagle populations in North America for many years. In Maine, where the rivers carried the highest concentrations of DDT, the eagles had the poorest nesting success. In Alaska, the reverse is true.

Just how DDT caused sterility in eagles remained a mystery until 1968 when it was discovered that DDT interferes with the bird's ability to manufacture calcium, a vital element in egg shells. Thin egg shells, which are so fragile they break in the normal incubation process before the eagle can fully develop, have now been found to be a major factor in the rising eagle mortality. Eagles, ospreys, peregrine falcons, brown pelicans, seagulls, and white-faced ibises are some of the birds that DDT appears to have added to a long list of birds facing extinction.

No one really knows what the eventual toll of birdlife from DDT and other chlorinated hydrocarbons will be. It seems certain that these poisons will be killing both birds and mammals for a long, long time.

The spectacular effects on aquatic birds of oil spills

around the world are all too familiar. If men can walk on the moon, it should be possible to devise ways of transporting oil from one place to another without these tragic losses of wildlife and valuable fuel. Again, these accidents are easy for all the world to see, whereas no one has ever seen a molecule of DDT with his naked eye. Will birds still be dying of insecticides when oil spills are almost a thing of the past?

In addition to the hunter who kills birds for recreation and food, raccoons which kill only for food, and pesticides which kill birds by accident, state and federal governments are deeply involved in the bird-killing business. Because the vast grain fields make perfect feeding grounds for millions of red-winged blackbirds, the United States Department of Agriculture and the Department of the Interior are spending millions of dollars trying to devise an efficient method to kill the red-wings. The same is true of great concentrations of starlings, house sparrows, and domestic pigeons.

There is a multitude of poisons already available that will kill birds. Experience with insecticides, however, has taught that poisons do not "stay put," nor do they necessarily affect only their special target. They may cause more damage than killing the species they were meant to kill. Scientists, therefore, are insisting that any bird poisons be thoroughly tested for side effects before they are put on the market.

In lieu of poisons, scientists are testing possible methods of scaring birds out of fields. They have learned that when one bird gives a call of fright or danger, the entire flock takes off. When these distress calls are recorded and amplified in a field, a fair measure of control is achieved.

Research is also progressing on development of a sterilant, a sort of birth control pill for birds which is added to their food. Still another drug causes a bird to temporarily behave very abnormally, uttering distress calls and carrying on in a manner which frightens its companions. This, too, holds promise of being a safe means to protect grain in fields and in livestock feeding lots.

Instead of resorting to poisons which kill not only blackbirds but doves, pheasants, hawks, cats, and dogs as well, a growing number of people ask if there is not

The environment of mockingbirds apparently has built-in population controls.

some environmental change they could bring about that would simply reduce the carrying capacity of the land for red-wings and starlings.

The environment of mockingbirds apparently has built-in population controls which keep the saucy clowns from having a population explosion. Something must kill about as many mockingbirds as are hatched each year. What it is, no one knows. If they did, perhaps it could be used to control blackbird populations. If people understood more about a bird's environment, it might be possible to control the overabundant species without resorting to poisons.

So far, at least, deliberate attempts to kill large numbers of "nuisance" birds seem to pose as much of a threat to other species, including humans, as to the unwanted birds.

Man's Effect on Birds

chapter nine

Since the days when man lived in caves, hunger and thirst have stalked him. Considering mankind as a whole, all three and one-half billion people, the situation in recent decades has grown steadily worse instead of better. Tonight, over half the people in the world will go to bed hungry. A look at some of yesterday's mistakes may help avoid similar ones in the future.

Birds have always been, and still are, a vital source of human food. Yet history is replete with instances in which man destroyed a bird that could have kept him from starvation. Unfortunately, much of this unwise action was not that of men driven to desperation by hunger. Often it simply arose from the false belief that *all* those birds could never disappear.

Take, for example, the passenger pigeon in North America. According to Mr. A. W. Shorger, the world's foremost authority on this now extinct species, the wild pigeon may have numbered about *three billion* at the time of Columbus' discovery of North America. No present-day land bird in the world approaches such abundance. At that time, probably about one-third of all the birds in North America were passenger pigeons.

That the flesh of the pigeons was delicious to eat is a matter of record. But this did not prevent the senseless, excessive slaughter of this valuable source of food. A single throw of a huge net over a cleared and baited area could capture over 1200 birds at one time. After half a dozen throws of such a net, 50 barrels of passenger pigeons worth a total of $650 were on their way to the nearest railroad station. Throughout history, a source of "instant wealth" such as this has often blinded the world's most intelligent mammal.

A lone example of the now-extinct passenger pigeon.

It should be pointed out, however, that incredible clouds of flying passenger pigeons at times blotted out the sun. There were so many birds that the mid-nineteenth century "pigeoner" could hardly have been expected to believe America would ever run out of them.

Everything the pigeons did was done in tremendous flocks. One great nesting area, near Petoskey, Michigan, was 12 miles wide and 40 miles long. Within this area, called a "nesting," a single tree might contain well over 100 nests.

Men came with wagons, armed with guns, clubs, axes, nets, and long poles to knock the plump, young squabs out of the nests. They cut down trees loaded with nests and collected the squabs, or fed them to the hogs which ran loose in the woods. Conversation within a nesting area was impossible. The roar of fluttering wings, cooing doves, breaking branches, and falling trees made it necessary for men to shout at each other when face-to-face. The ground and the clothing of the pigeoners were whitewashed with pigeon excrement. This carnage continued, day after day, from May until August. The pocketbooks of merchants, railroaders, and pigeoners grew fat on fat birds.

The early naturalists who first realized that the number of pigeons slaughtered in a season exceeded the number of young produced sought in vain for legislation to control the harvest. Even the feeble laws they were able to have passed were not enforced. Then, as now, public officials, judges, and juries were reluctant to enforce laws which curbed the rapid conversion of a natural resource into dollars. Then, as now, however, the general public gradually became aware that changes were taking place in the environment of birds. These changes meant that something of value in their own lives would soon be gone forever.

In the case of the passenger pigeon, public efforts to save the bird were too little and too late. For too many years, the nets, clubs, and guns had killed the squabs before they could mature and produce more pigeons. But had the killing been stopped in time, the birds still could not have survived without thousands of square miles of hardwood forest in which to nest, without millions of bushels of acorns, weed seeds, or man-raised grain for food.

Had people known in time, they could have controlled the gun and net. But they could not have stopped the axe and plow, the replacement of forests by agriculture, the spread of steel and concrete, or the advent of smog and DDT. The fate of the passenger pigeon was sealed by a combination of human hunger, greed, lack of knowledge about the conservation of the bird, and America's westward expansion.

The extinction of several other bird species is not as complicated. In the case of the great auk, hungry sailors found the ridiculously tame, black and white, flightless, penguinlike bird too tempting to resist. Armed only with clubs but hungry for fresh, red meat, the nineteenth-century seamen invaded the islands of the North Atlantic and converted the goose-sized, trusting birds to stew meat. Some use was also made of their feathers.

On these remote islands, there were no laws to protect the great auks, and no officers to enforce the laws had there been any. The attitude of the invader was, "I'll get mine while the getting is good." As far as is known, the world's last pair of great auks was clubbed to death on June 3, 1844. The cause of the birds' demise lay in an evolutionary history which had rendered them flightless. This inability to fly, combined with their lack of fear of those other two-legged creatures who stood and walked erect, spelled their doom.

A somewhat different case is the now almost extinct Eskimo curlew. The curlew had one trait in common with passenger pigeons. It migrated in great, compact flocks. Early accounts of the tremendous slaughter of game birds by market hunters show the vulnerability of these shorebirds to mass shooting. Had the curlews made their spring migration from Argentina across the midwestern prairies of America in small, scattered flocks, they might still be abundant. But as in the case of the pigeons and the auks, the curlews' gregarious nature meant easy money and abundant food to people as long as the huge flocks continued to fly.

The enterprise of killing wildlife species for profit and selling the game to consumers was called market hunting. By the time it was outlawed, great flocks of Eskimo curlews had disappeared, perhaps never to return. For 20 years, no curlew was seen. Then a lone bird was sighted on Galveston Island, Texas, in March of 1959. For the next three years, a straggler appeared at Galveston in the spring, but none has been seen since. Recently, a lone curlew specimen discovered in the freezer of a resident of Barbados, British West Indies, was hardly cause for rejoicing. It is evidence, however, that at least one curlew made it from the Arctic shores almost back to Argentina.

From these few observations by a handful of individuals, it is impossible to say whether or not the Eskimo curlew can be saved from extinction. Their nesting habitat lies somewhere on the barren Arctic tundra. It is not known exactly where. Hopefully, man has not yet been able to destroy this habitat. There are no cities on the Arctic tundra, no paved roads, no vast farms devoted to a single crop, no bare, plowed fields that stretch for miles offering the curlews a landscape without food or cover. As far as is known, the curlew's nesting environment may contain the same amount and kinds of plants that were there 100 years ago. It is almost certain, however, that this environment also contains DDT because this poison now has world-wide distribution. Whether the concentration of pesticides has reached lethal levels for Eskimo curlews no one knows.

Laws have been passed to protect from hunting all shorebirds that even resemble curlews. Treaties with Canada and Mexico extend this protection to most of North America where the greatest shooting abuses formerly existed. Rigid protection in regions where the bird is known to occur seems to be all that can be done for the Eskimo curlew. There is no assurance that it is not already too late.

For the curlew, the exploding guns of North America

have been silenced to help save this species. But the exploding human population around the world is a threat to all wildlife. Can the dangers from poisons and from people, as well as from hunting, be brought under control? The survival of many species of birds and other wildlife, including man, depends on it.

Fortunately, in the country, in the city, and in the forest, many bird species alive today are in no immediate danger of extinction. For them, there is much that can be done. There is much, in fact, that has already been done.

People here and now are faced with the task of preserving an environment which will not push additional birds, mammals, and man over the brink to extinction. Once enough people realize it is to their own advantage to maintain an environment suitable for birds, some of today's policies, which are of temporary benefit but unwise from the environmental standpoint, may be reversed.

With no thought of feeding himself, man has unwittingly changed the environment of the heath hen, the Carolina parakeet, the peregrine falcon, the ivory-billed woodpecker, and the brown pelican. Of the seventy-six bird species which are completely extinct, and the long list of others on the verge of extinction, many were victims of man-made changes in which no harm to birds was intended.

Admittedly, the raptors, or flesh eaters, were persecuted because people did not understand the relationship between predators and their prey. People know better today. Most states not only have stopped the payment of bounties on eagles, hawks, and owls, they have passed laws to protect these birds. Both bald and golden eagles are protected by federal law, and there is reason to hope such nationwide protection will soon be extended to all birds of prey.

Enforcement of these laws is still not what it should be. Many hunters, and even a few game wardens, lack adequate information. They do not fully understand that while a raptor may kill a few pheasants, it is still of benefit to the pheasant family as a whole. Fortunately, education in this area is steadily changing for the better.

Practically all of the songbirds, both the seed eaters and the insectivores, are protected by state or federal laws. Passing good laws to protect birds from the net, gun, and trap is a tedious process. Adequate enforcement of good laws requires even more time; time to train enforcement officers, and time to educate the judges and the ordinary citizens who serve on the juries about the wisdom and reasoning behind the laws. All too often, a judge who is not aware of the part birds and other wildlife play in the environment of men levies token fines for flagrant violations involving the killing and/or capturing of wild creatures. This encourages further violations and demoralizes enforcement officers.

The twentieth century has seen encouraging strides in the field of wildlife legislation and enforcement. These achievements, slow as they are in coming, are minimal compared to the task that lies ahead—that of restoring an environment in which birds can live and in which people cannot only live but have something to live *for.*

Scientists studying the health of human beings are increasingly aware that birds are a sort of "window" through which people may perceive their own needs as well as threats to human welfare. Yesterday's coal miner, unable to detect odorless, colorless, dangerous gases, kept an anxious eye on the caged canary he carried into the mine for this purpose. The canary, being very sensitive to deadly gases men could neither see nor smell, served as an environmental danger signal. If the bird showed signs of distress, the coal miner quickly withdrew from that area.

Birds are providing similar danger signals in today's changing world. Long before the public became alarmed over mercury contamination in seafood, the brown pelican, a fish eater, disappeared over most of its range. Scientists are now conducting studies to determine the effects of chemicals on pelicans and other fish eaters, including man.

The State of New York, alarmed by the very high level of DDT found in human mothers' milk, in 1971, outlawed the use of DDT and related poisons. Although New York led all other states in this regard, its native peregrine falcon had all but disappeared before New Yorkers became alarmed.

Great Britain outlawed the use of persistent pesticides in 1964, before America awoke to the danger. Apparently British bird watchers "got the message" from their bird populations and were able to alert members of Parliament before American legislators began to deal with pesticides problems.

The world-wide spread of chlorinated hydrocarbons

is only one change in the environment that affects the food and shelter of birds. Some other changes are for the better. For example, in 1872, in the northwest corner of the state of Wyoming, an area of great scenic beauty and a wealth of plants, mammals, and birds, called Yellowstone, became America's first national park. Over the years, scenic areas have been added to the National Park System until, in 1970, there were over thirty-five parks, comprising over 14 million acres. In addition, hundreds of state and city parks have been set aside in which the habitats of birds are relatively undisturbed.

Of even more direct benefit is the great system of private, state, and national wildlife refuges across the continent of North America. One of the earliest wildlife sanctuaries came about through the deep concern of a few citizens over the devastating slaughter of egrets, especially in south Florida. During the nesting season these snow-white herons develop beautiful plumes called *aigrettes.* At that time, these feathers were worth their weight in gold as ornaments for ladies' hats. It resembled the passenger pigeon story all over again, but this time, enough people raised enough money in time to buy enough land to protect a breeding colony of birds. This association of wildlife protectors eventually became the National Audubon Society.

Mr. Guy Bradley, the first warden hired by the Audubon Society, in 1904, was deliberately killed by plume hunters. The millinery industry and the market hunters who collected egrets for them swore that no one would

About 1900, a fashion for plumed hats almost caused the extinction of the beautiful American egret.

The National Audubon Society helped to pass a law to protect the egrets from plume hunters.

be allowed to interfere with their "right" to trade wild birds for dollars. A small, but determined, group of citizens thought otherwise. They saw no reason why the world should lose a great wealth of natural beauty for the hats of vain women and the pocketbooks of a few greedy men.

Today, snowy egrets and all members of the heron family are protected by state and federal laws. The birds have regained their losses in a gratifying manner. The land purchased for their use by the founders of the Audubon Society is now part of the great Everglades National Park in Florida.

Unfortunately, the drastic changes threatening Everglades National Park today are typical of those facing every wildlife haven: be it a great national wildlife refuge, a small city park, a national forest, or private bird sanctuary. Every acre of open space that is not already devoted to agriculture, highways, houses, or industry is under surveillance by someone bent on putting it to commerical use.

In 1970, it took a nationwide protest to prevent the destruction of Everglades National Park to make way for a monstrous jetport planned for the park's northern boundary. This great community of tropical plants and animals, which exists nowhere else in the world, has been at least temporarily saved from water and air pollution and the noise of jumbo jets.

Several years before the jetport menace, this huge natural park had been almost completely destroyed by a grandiose drainage system constructed by the United

States Army Corps of Engineers. The excessive cost of this project, to taxpayers and to Everglades wildlife, is now coming to light. Consequently, the Corps is now required by law to have studies made of the possible impact on wildlife before starting future water control projects.

Changes wrought by man in the Everglades are typical of those in every state. Now there is growing public awareness of the hidden costs of superhighways that are forced through wildlife sanctuaries, forests, and parks; and of giant power plants that change the air, water, and travel lanes used by birds.

Not all environmental changes are detrimental. It is accidentally of benefit to seagulls when growing garbage dumps provide them with an unusual food supply. As a

Unsightly garbage dumps provide a food supply for seagulls, enabling them to increase their numbers in some areas.

result, the nesting colonies of the scavenging gulls along the coast of New England have expanded so much that the gulls are crowding out the nesting terns.

On the positive side, not all beneficial changes are accidental. Enough is known about the needs of various game and songbirds to provide these birds with better food and cover than is ordinarily available. On the Paul J. Rainey Wildlife Sanctuary in Louisiana, for example, wardens annually burn thousands of acres of dry, mature, wire grass. This controlled burning makes the new tender shoots and roots that follow available to the wintering blue geese. Otherwise, the geese could not feed on the thick, dry grass and would have to look for food on cattle ranches where the birds are not welcome.

In the forests of America and Europe, foresters make judicious use of their saws, removing some mature trees to allow the sunlight to reach the forest floor. New plants which cannot tolerate shade are thus encouraged. Their growth provides food and cover for grouse, thrushes, and other forest birds.

For the small Kirtland's warbler, people in Michigan provide a very specific kind of nesting habitat consisting of young jack pine trees. Simply because people admire and enjoy this attractive bird, and because it is part of their lives, they take special care to maintain the only kind of habitat in which the Kirtland's warbler will nest. If the jack pines were not periodically cut or burned, the entire forest would mature, the number of young trees would decline, and with the trees would go the last of the world's Kirtland's warblers.

Man's Effect on Birds

Looking back over the last century, there is a record of men who killed and sold certain birds until they became extinct. There were governments that paid bounties on hawks, owls, and eagles, then gradually switched to protecting these birds in the light of new knowledge. There were men who built cities, pastures, and roads out of the forest, and mindlessly eliminated forest birds in the process. There were farmers who turned the great sea of waving prairie grasses into one huge cornfield and eliminated the prairie chicken.

Within recent times, the spectacular die-off of such species as the brown pelican, the osprey, and the American eagle has made people pause to contemplate and then move to counteract the effect of world-wide pollution on birds and men.

Various birds have made marvelous adaptations to different environments. In spite of their remarkable attributes and adaptability evolved through millions of years of evolution, there is still one process no bird can perform. A bird cannot think for itself.

If mankind can only learn enough about the changing world of birds, man may still be able to stop pollution and to restore the great diversity of plants and animals that is necessary to keep the planet livable.

Birds cannot think for themselves, but people can.

A Word About Birds and Bird-Watching

afterword

Bird study has become an absorbing hobby for millions of people from every nation and every walk of life, for men and women, old and young, rich and poor. If you like feathered creatures, you will find you have lots of company. Birders in your home town, whether it is Nome, London, or Moscow, will willingly share their knowledge and lore with young people.

Perhaps no science has benefited more from amateur effort than ornithology. Great contributions have been made by nonprofessionals. Mr. C. L. Broley, a retired banker nearly 70 years of age, banded more than a thousand eaglets, climbing many a tall Florida tree in order to reach their nests. From his work, ornithologists learned that the bald eagle disperses northward over a broad area in the United States and the Maritime Provinces of Canada.

If you live in a rural or suburban area, bird study begins in your front yard or, if you wish, on your windowsill. Planting shrubs and evergreens for shelter and providing regular food and water will make your yard a feature attraction for perhaps fifty or more different bird species. Instructions for building various kinds of birdhouses can usually be obtained by writing to your state conservation department or to the National Audubon Society, 950 Third Avenue, New York, N.Y. 10022.

The absence of bird habitats around city homes can frequently be offset by a museum of natural history, maintained by the city or a university. Study of the displays there will pay dividends when you do have an opportunity to go out to the marsh, seashore, fields, forests, parks, or wildlife sanctuaries.

If you can get close enough, all you really need for bird study are good eyes and ears. Two pieces of equipment that may increase your fun are binoculars and a camera. Simple seven-power binoculars will bring a bird seven times closer. In the field binoculars are almost essential. The best way to decide on which type of binoculars and camera to use is to check with experienced birders. Tape recorders and phonograph records may also be of great help in learning bird songs, although a day in the field with a friend who knows bird songs is equally profitable.

Simply being able to accurately identify birds is the beginning of wisdom in the out-of-doors. For this purpose, the foremost of modern artist/ornithologists is Roger Tory Peterson, whose field guides cover all continents. The pictures in Peterson's *Field Guide to the Birds* are accurate, easy to use, complete, and beautiful.

No matter what books, binoculars, or other aids are available, once you are out in the field and spot your first bird, the excitement begins. You will want to take careful note of the color, size, shape—looking for such "trademarks" as white outer tail feathers, a line through the eye, a crest on the head, a long straight beak or a short and hooked one. Once you have identified the bird, you will be looking with the eye of an artist and you will see a different world from that day on.

As the number of birds you can identify grows, spotting new species will bring a thrill of discovery. Most of us have a curiosity about animal life which birding satisfies. Making a list of the birds you have seen, and the locations where you saw them, is a start. When you add notes on the numbers seen, terrain, weather, date, behavior (whether singing, nesting, courting, or migrating) you have made a contribution to ornithology.

American Birds, a bimonthly journal devoted to the birds of North America published by the National Audubon Society in collaboration with the U.S. Fish & Wildlife Service, is widely used by scientists and depends almost entirely on the observations of amateur birders. The local bird study group nearest you probably participates in the annual Christmas Bird Count, the Spring Breeding Season Census, the January Inventory of Waterfowl, and similar functions which are fun for the participants and of value to science. Proficiency in bird identification is essential for a career in conservation.

A chapter of the National Audubon Society, or a local bird club, can be found in almost every state or Canadian province, especially in the larger cities. You are welcome at their meetings, lectures, and field trips, through which you can broaden your interest and experience. Most groups publish newsletters or journals. Their meetings often feature motion pictures or slides of birds. Audubon Screen Tours also present outstanding wildlife films and lectures. For help in locating these, consult the Conservation Directory of the National Wildlife Federation, your state conservation department, the library, or newspaper of either your home town or the nearest large city.

To identify a bird is to make a friend. Its song or color enhances your everyday world. It whets your interest in other birds. You become a "bird watcher."

The man who calls himself a hunter, but who is really only a "bird shooter" confines his interest to the species he hunts, learning little besides where to find them during the season. The true bird hunter is often also a bird watcher. His sport permeates his life and he is constantly increasing his knowledge of birds, which may explain why an ardent duck hunter, such as Dudley Mills of New York, or a quail hunter, such as Robert Brown of Missouri, appears on the Board of Directors of the National Audubon Society. Local bird clubs across the country are fortunate to have many knowledgeable hunter-bird watchers as members.

Dr. Aldo Leopold (1886–1948), often referred to as the father of game management in North America, was an ardent bird watcher. He knew as much about the lives and times of prothonotary warblers as he did about ruffed grouse and woodcock, which he hunted.

As an artist, John James Audubon (1785–1851) will live forever in America. But his skill with the brush was matched by the great contribution he made in writing his *Ornithological Biography* (1839). In this book he describes the birds he saw as he floated down the Mississippi, pushing into the swamps on either side; as he traveled through the forests along the Ohio River; and as he journeyed along the rich Atlantic coast of South Carolina. His accounts are some of the most complete and accurate that have been published to this day.

John J. Audubon's skill as a hunter was nearly equal to his skill with the brush and pen. Hunting increased Audubon's knowledge of birds: their life histories, songs, habitats, and feeding habits. This information made possible his great contribution to our own knowledge of the environment as it was in the early 1800s.

John J. Audubon recorded the world of birds as it was in 1839.

Those who hunt birds for food or sport number about 16 million in the United States; those who use only binoculars and cameras for their bird-watching number slightly less. Both groups of bird lovers occasionally join forces in the war to protect the environment of birds. All too often, however, they spend their energy in bitter argument over man's right to kill birds and mammals.

The bird watcher contends that the hunter, at least in England and America, no longer needs to kill for food. Yet hunting gives pleasure to thousands of people. There is abundant evidence that *well regulated* hunting is not damaging to bird populations. In years of good production, when waterfowl populations are large due to abundant rainfall on the prairie nesting grounds, hunting restrictions are relaxed. In years of drought and consequent low production, restrictions are tightened.

Greater public awareness and concern are needed to protect and preserve natural habitats. For example, the law to protect the bald eagle from shooting was passed in 1940, but legislation that will really stop the use of DDT around the world, which both hunters and nonhunters support, is still a long way off. Both bird watcher and hunter work toward the preservation of habitats and both join forces in fighting pollution from oil, automobile exhaust, and industrial wastes.

In the words of William Cullen Byrant (1794–1878):

"To him who in the love of Nature holds
Communion with her visible forms, she speaks
A various language. . . ."

glossary

aigrettes: Ornamental tufts of upright plumes, especially the tail feathers of an egret.

algae: Any of several groups of simple green plants, chiefly aquatic, that range from one-celled, usually microscopic, forms to larger multicellular forms.

altricial: Helpless and naked when hatched, needing parental care.

barb: One of the many parallel filaments projecting from the main shaft of a feather.

barbule: One of the small projections fringing the edges of the barbs of a feather.

biologist: A person who is trained in or specializes in biology, the science of life and life processes.

botulism: A disease of the nervous system, often fatal, caused by botulin produced by the bacterium *Clostridium botulinum.*

carrying capacity: The maximum number of a given organism a given area can support.

chlorinated-hydrocarbon: A poisonous chemical compound containing chlorine, hydrogen, and carbon.

community: A group of plants or animals or both, living in a specific region.

conservation: Official supervision to preserve natural resources, such as topsoil, forests, and waterways.

contour feather: Any of the outermost feathers of a bird, forming the visible body contour and plumage.

crop: A pouchlike enlargement of a bird's throat in which food is held or partially digested.

DDT [abbreviation for d(ichloro)d(iphenyl)t(richloroethane)]: A colorless chlorinated-hydrocarbon, used as an insecticide, which is poisonous to man and animals when swallowed or absorbed through the skin.

detergent: A cleansing substance made from synthetic chemical compounds rather than from fats and lye used in making soap.

down: Fine, soft, fluffy feathers forming the first plumage of a young bird and underlying the contour feathers of an adult bird.

ecology: The branch of biology that deals with the relations between living organisms and their environment.

embryo: An organism in its early stages of development, as before emergence from the egg.

environment: All the conditions surrounding and affecting the development of an organism.

eutrophication: When an increase of mineral and organic nutrients, in a body of water, results in such a dense growth of plants and animals that the water is depleted of oxygen when they die and start to decay.

extinction: The act or process of becoming extinct—that is, no longer existing in a living form; having died out.

filoplumes: Hairlike feathers having few or no barbs.

gallinaceous: Pertaining to or resembling the domestic fowls, such as chickens, pheasants, turkeys, and grouse.

gizzard: An enlargement of the alimentary canal in birds, often having dense muscular walls; seeds are digested in it with the aid of fine grit.

gonad: A gland that produces reproductive cells; an ovary or testis.

habitat: The area or type of environment in which an animal or plant normally lives.

incubation: The act of incubating, which is to keep eggs warm to promote embryonic development and hatching.

insectivorous: Adapted to feeding on insects.

mammal: A warm-blooded animal that has a backbone and hair and that nourishes its young with milk.

mandible: In birds, either the upper or lower part of the bill.

migration: The action or an act of migrating, which is to move seasonally from one region to another.

monoculture: The use of land to grow only one type of crop.

ornithologist: A scientist who studies birds.

pabulum: Any substance that gives nourishment; food.

parasite: An organism that lives, feeds, and is sheltered in or on another organism.

pesticide: Any chemical that is used to kill pests, especially insects and rodents.

population: All the organisms of the same kind that live in a given area.

predator: An animal that captures and eats other animals.

prey: Any creature hunted or seized for food.

raptor: A bird of prey.

sanctuary: A reserved area in which animals or birds are protected from hunting or other molestation.

scavenger: An animal that feeds on dead animal flesh or other decaying organic matter.

shaft: The main stem of a feather.

talon: The claw of a bird of prey.

toxin: Any of certain poisonous compounds that are produced by microorganisms, plants, or animals, and cause diseases or other adverse physiological reactions.

tundra: A treeless area between the ice cap and the tree line of arctic regions, having a permanently frozen subsoil and supporting low-growing vegetation, such as lichens, mosses, and stunted shrubs.

vane: The flattened, weblike part of a feather, consisting of a series of barbs on either side of the shaft.

wetlands: Land on which water stands at least part of the year.

books for further reading

Suggested Reading

Allen, Robert Porter. *The Flame Birds.* New York: Dodd, Mead & Co., 1947.

———. *The Giant Golden Book of Birds.* New York: Golden Press, 1962.

Austing, G. Ronald. *The World of the Red-Tailed Hawk.* Philadelphia: J. B. Lippincott Company, 1964.

———. and Holt, John B., Jr. *The World of the Great Horned Owl.* Philadelphia: J. B. Lippincott Company, 1966.

Cosgrove, Margaret. *Eggs & What Happens Inside Them.* New York: Dodd, Mead & Co., 1966.

Cruickshank, Allan, and Cruickshank, Helen. *1,001 Questions Answered About Birds.* New York: Dodd, Mead & Co., 1958.

Darling, Louis. *The Gull's Way.* New York: William Morrow & Co., 1965.

Hochbaum, H. Albert. *The Canvasback on a Prairie Marsh.* Washington, D.C.: The American Wildlife Institute, 1944.

Kieran, John. *An Introduction to Birds.* Garden City, New York: Doubleday & Company, 1965.

Lewellen, John Bryan. *Birds and Planes: How They Fly.* New York: T. Y. Crowell Company, 1953.

Books for Further Reading

McCoy, J. J. *The Hunt for the Whooping Cranes.* New York: Lothrop, Lee & Shepard Co., 1966.

McNulty, Faith. *The Whooping Crane.* New York: E. P. Dutton & Co., 1966.

Murphy, Robert. *The Peregrine Falcon.* Boston: Houghton Mifflin Company, 1963.

Peterson, Roger Tory. *A Field Guide to the Birds.* Boston: Houghton Mifflin Company, 1947.

———. *The Birds.* New York: Time-Life Books, Time Inc., 1970.

Robbins, Chandler S.; Bruun, Bertel; and Zim, Herbert S. *Birds of North America.* New York: Golden Press, 1966.

Bibliography

Austin, Oliver L., Jr. *Song Birds of the World.* New York: Golden Press, 1967.

———. *Water and Marsh Birds of the World.* New York: Golden Press, 1967.

Cockrum, Lendell E., and McCauley, William J. *Zoology.* Philadelphia: W. B. Saunders Company, 1965.

Commoner, Barry. *Science & Survival.* New York: The Viking Press, 1966.

Gilliard, E. Thomas. *Living Birds of the World.* Garden City, New York: Doubleday & Company, 1958.

Hochbaum, H. Albert. *Travels and Traditions of Waterfowl.* Minneapolis: The University of Minnesota Press, 1955.

Linduska, Joseph P., et al. *Waterfowl Tomorrow.* Washington, D.C.: The United States Department of the Interior, 1964.

Pearson, Thomas Gilbert. *Adventures in Bird Protection.* New York: D. Appleton-Century Company, 1937.

Reilly, Edgar M., Jr. *The Audubon Illustrated Handbook of American Birds.* New York: McGraw-Hill Book Company, 1968.

Roberts, Thomas S. *The Birds of Minnesota.* Minneapolis: The University of Minnesota Press, 1932.

Sprunt, Alexander, IV, and Zim, Herbert S. *Gamebirds.* New York: Golden Press, 1961.

Stefferud, Alfred, et al. *Birds in Our Lives.* Washington, D.C.: The United States Department of the Interior, 1966.

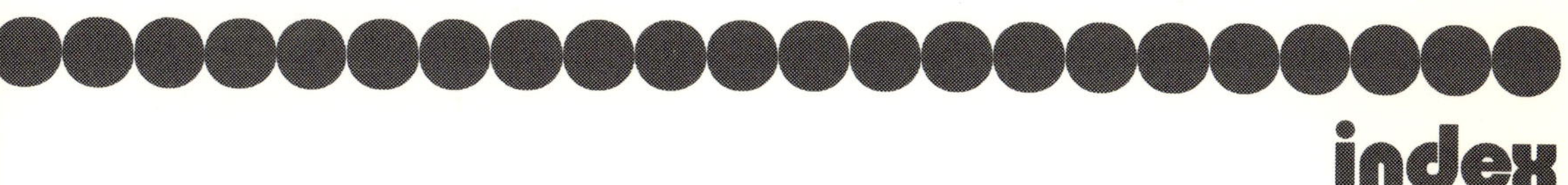

index

(Page numbers in italics refer to illustrations.)